in the Egyptian Wilderness

Bedouin Life in the Egyptian Wilderness

JOSEPH J. HOBBS
FOREWORD BY LEO TREGENZA

University of Texas Press Austin

First paperback printing, 1992

Requests for permission to reproduce material from this work should
be sent to Permissions, University of Texas Press, Box 7819, Austin,
Texas 78713-7819.

⊗ The paper used in this publication meets the minimum requirements of American National Standard for Information Sciences—
Permanence of Paper for Printed Library Materials, ANSI Z39.48-1984.

Library of Congress Cataloging-in-Publication Data
Hobbs, Joseph J. (Joseph John), 1956–
  Bedouin life in the Egyptian wilderness / Joseph J. Hobbs ; with a
foreword by Leo Tregenza. — 1st ed.
    p.   cm.
  Bibliography: p.
  Includes index.
  ISBN 0-292-71556-0 (alk. paper)
  1. Maʿaza (Arab tribe) 2. Eastern Desert (Egypt)—Social
conditions. 3. Eastern Desert (Egypt)—Description and travel.
4. Hobbs, Joseph J. (Joseph John), 1956– —Journeys—Egypt—
Eastern Desert. I. Title.
DT72.B4H6 1989
305.8'9270623—dc20   89-32001
                                                               CIP

ISBN 0-292-70789-4 pbk.

For My Family

Contents

Illustrations

Maps

Photographs following page 48

Foreword

It was natural, I suppose, that Joe Hobbs should ask me to write a foreword to his book because, although nearly half a century separates our activities in the area he describes, his journeys and experiences were remarkably similar to mine. Having read my two books on the subject, he continued and widened the work I had done in the Eastern Desert of Egypt. The material reason for my going there was an investigation into its Greek, Roman, and other antiquities, but Joe's much broader object was to go into the past history of the Ma'aza tribe; to describe all aspects of the present life and conditions of its small Khushmaan clan, especially the difficulties they face, in that fascinating part of Egypt where they live now; and to evaluate their prospects for survival. We both traveled many hundreds of miles on foot, on different occasions, with our Khushmaan guides, covering almost the whole of that extensive territory in our search for the data and other information we wished to acquire. Of immense help was our guides' accurate and very detailed knowledge of the terrain, but Joe with his most fluent command of the Arabic language was able also to probe more deeply into their attitude to their surroundings and into their outlook on life in general, a much more difficult thing to do.

What delighted me most in his revival of interest in the Eastern Desert was that Joe's reactions to his experiences there were very much akin to my own. We both enjoyed them immensely. We were fully accepted into the nomads' way of life because they knew how much we appreciated and identified ourselves with it. We regarded it to be a privilege to be accepted in this way. Any idea of patronizing on our part would have been an insult to them and utterly absurd. For us it was a welcome and refreshing escape from the complexities and much of the artificiality of the more "developed" world.

In his treatment of the earlier history of the Ma'aza, Joe does not spare them an account of its uglier features, the cruelty and the killings in the raids that had been a regular feature of nearly all Arab tribes for many years. But for the Ma'aza that is a thing of the past, and the book deals almost wholly with the Khushmaan clan, not more than about a thousand people altogether, in their settled and now officially recognized territory in the Eastern Desert, where they are at complete freedom to move with their domestic animals in pursuit of their pastoral life. That freedom, as they frequently told us, is their most cherished possession, in spite of the hardships they suffer in periods of prolonged drought. Joe's description of the area is so detailed and authoritative because the Khushmaan are fully acquainted with its geography, all its wild animals and birds and plants, and the many ways in which they use them to sustain their livelihood. Their territory is of course quite cut off from the rest of the Arab world with its internal feuds and external struggles. They know and care very little of what is happening in that world.

The research value of this book will be obvious to the reader. I doubt if any other investigation of this kind has ever gone so thoroughly into its subject. Particularly interesting is the way Joe's subtle questioning reveals the Khushmaan rather "psychological" outlook on their homeland, as, for instance, his analysis of their feeling for places of all kinds, especially those that have human associations attached to them. He tells us of a little stretch of wadi, with an acacia tree in it, that was the "home" of a man who spent a long time there and made sure the tree came to no harm. In the Arab view that tree and that man are now also an intrinsic part of the identity of the place. "It," quite simply, is a combination of all three. Our modern existential philosophy might perhaps find something of interest to it here! There are other rather similar examples. The main gorge of Jebel Shaayib, the highest mountain of the area, is called Showak because Showak was the name of the man who many years ago made it his "home," hanging his few belongings perhaps to the branches of a tree there. There is a well-known wadi named al-Atrash, which in Arabic means "the deaf one," as a man who once lived there was deaf.

Another example of this Khushmaan feeling for their landscape, although it is not in Joe's book, is, I think, worth recording. Some of his guides were the sons of the ones I had, still not born or babes in arms when I was in the desert. They had heard stories from their fathers of the journeys they had had with me, and when they learned from Joe that I was still alive, one of them sent me a dictated letter begging me to come back into the desert to visit them again, adding (an amazing idea coming from such untutored sons of the desert) that the mountains and valleys that were so well known to me still mourned my absence. For them, although they had never seen me, I was still a real part of their landscape. It took me back to the myth of Orpheus and a few similar examples in the literature of Greece and Rome.

Inevitably in his endless talk with his guides, especially in the long hours of darkness, Joe raises the subject of the stars and the part they play in the nomads' lives. They chart their course by them when they are on the move by night, for when the day's heat has gone in that fairly high altitude the stars are always clear and unclouded overhead. Seated on the sand around their campfire at the close of day and talking perhaps for hours together at their bread making and their evening meal, they look up at the heavens now and then to see how the night is progressing, to "read the time." They lie asleep then on the open ground close to the last warmth of the dead ashes of the fire, and in the profound silence of the night the stars begin to acquire an incredible brilliance and nearness above them. This lifelong and intimate contact with the stars seems to give a deeper dimension and an extra dignity to their lives. The Arabs have always regarded the stars as the majestic work of God, and it gives them a finer resignation, a more detached view of life than most people can acquire. Even the death of loved ones must seem less bitter to them, for on the move or at rest each night in their desert solitude they have the starry universe for house and home, the greatest place of all, where the barrier between the living and the dead is already more than half borne away.

My relations with my Khushmaan guides were among the finest male friendships I have formed in the course of a long life, and I know Joe feels much the same way about them. For me they are still alive, constantly in my thoughts, an essential part of the attractive desert landscape that is their home. They are poor men, judged by the standards most of us are accustomed to, but poor only in the material possessions of this world. For close companion to that poverty is their inborn belief in the divine governance of the world. As Suliman said to me, "Young or getting on in years, we are all subject to the will of God." As the days and weeks of our long walks together went on, that philosophy seemed to join with the bright sunlight to cast its spell around our lives, and certainly the experiences I shared with them have enriched my own life ever since.

What kind of future are we heading for in our modern world, with its intensive and ever-increasing use of machinery of all kinds, its population problems, the steady encroachment of roads and new towns on our natural landscape everywhere, and who knows what disasters the spread of applied science may have in store for us? All the more reason therefore to hope that some regions of our planet are not involved in that process. It would be a great pity if the way of life so well described in the following pages eventually comes to an end. I hope this book, especially the chapter on the conservation policy of the Khushmaan for their natural resources, will be a real help in its preservation.

LEO TREGENZA
Paul, Cornwall
2 May 1988

Preface

From 1982 to 1984, and in the autumn of 1986, I had the good fortune to be the guest of the Ma'aza Bedouins who live in Egypt's Eastern Desert. I was studying the nomads' perceptions of their environment, working toward a doctorate in geography at the University of Texas at Austin. My status among the nomads was as the "way-fellow" (*rafiig*) of Saalih 'Ali Suwaylim, a man in his early forties who had earned a reputation among his peers as an outstanding naturalist. Saalih was my principal guide, mentor, and informant and became my close friend.

Saalih did not set limits on what I could learn but encouraged me to know as many of his kinsmen and see as much of their land as possible. For outsiders there is very little information available about the cultures, antiquities, plants, and animals of the Eastern Desert, so that virtually everything we came across was of interest. Saalih typically set as our destination of a day's or week's journey a particular mountain peak, wadi, water source, rare plant, or site of antiquity. He always routed the trip for maximum contact with his kinspeople, and visiting people became the exclusive goal of many journeys.

Saalih's enthusiasm as guide and teacher, the willingness of his kinsmen to share their world with me, and their interest in mine, made these travels into journeys of mutual discovery between the nomads and me. This book relates what we learned together. On paper and audio tapes, I constantly recorded and recounted what the Bedouins told me, often evoking discussions about natural history, family history, and world view which were clearly as interesting to the Bedouins as to me. I have preserved the original tape recordings, and where appropriate have translated the Bedouins' words directly into this text, where they form numerous block quotations. My second guide and teacher was Muhammad Umbaarak, a man of extraordinary energy and dignity who died in 1987 at the age of about seventy-five. His words are preserved in this text and in the writings of Leo Tregenza, the remarkable Englishman with whom Muhammad traveled in 1947 and 1949 and who became my mentor and friend in the mid-1980s.

My deepest thanks are to these men, Saalih ʿAli, Muhammad Umbaarak, and Leo Tregenza. Too many Khushmaan men and women to mention by name, but notably Musallim Sulimaan, ʿAbd al-Dhaahir Sulimaan, Umtayr Muhammad, and their families, helped me.

In Cairo, Dr. Loutfy Boulos of the National Research Center and Dr. Mohammed Kassas and Mr. Loutfy Mohsen of the Herbarium of Cairo University facilitated my research and carefully identified my plant specimens. The late Dr. Harry Hoogstraal, Mr. Ibrahim Helmy, and Mr. Sherif Tewfig of the U.S. Naval Medical Research Unit No. 3 encouraged me to do desert research and identified many of my field specimens. I am grateful to Dr. Dale Osborn for inspiring some of my early trips in the Eastern Desert. Dr. John Swanson of the American University in Cairo was a pillar of personal support. The Fulbright office and the American Research Center in Egypt helped secure official permits for my research. Red Sea Governor General Yusef Afifi and his aides, Mr. Nusaari, Mr. Dandaraawi, Mr. Muhammed al-Bishaari, and Muhammed "al-Shurta" of the Red Sea Governorate in Hurghada, finally made this research possible.

I am indebted to the Fulbright-Hays Doctoral Dissertation Research Abroad Program and to the Graduate School, Center for Middle Eastern Studies and Department of Geography at the University of Texas at Austin, for funding my fieldwork. Drs. Robin Doughty, Ian Manners, Robert Holz, and Robert Fernea of the University of Texas helped me through every stage leading to this book. So did Steve Goodman, a brilliant field naturalist of the University of Michigan Museum of Zoology. I am grateful to Edward Khounganian for contributing a base map after which the maps in this text were patterned. My family, especially my grandfather E. O. Rhodes, has been a great inspiration in every stage of my work. In meeting Saalih and some of my other desert companions, my family members brought us all closer together. Finally, I thank my wife, Cindy, who encouraged me to keep writing and helped edit the manuscript.

I have devised a system which affords a reasonable phonetic rendition of the Arabic spoken by the nomads, while not confusing the non-Arabic-speaking reader; for example, I have not differentiated between the "hard" and "soft" *h*. I have kept most of the romanized place names the reader might encounter in published maps and texts but used this phonetic system for all other place names. The Bedouins have scores of names for types of topographic features, but I have distilled these as "wadi" to designate any drainage, and "jebel" for any elevation. The terms "Arab," which is the word the Bedouins use to distinguish themselves from farming and city folk, "Bedouin," and "nomad" are used synonymously. "Khushaymi" means a member of the Khushmaan clan; "Maʿazi," a member of the Maʿaza tribe; "Bishari," a member of the Bisharin tribe; and "ʿAbadi," a member of the ʿAbabda tribe. The exchange rate quoted for Egyptian pounds and American dollars is the average figure for 1982–1984, before the pound was devalued. I use English, Bedouin, and Latin names, in that order, to identify plants and animals; however, common English names, especially for plants, often do not exist. Appendix 1 is a thorough inventory of available Bedouin, English, and Latin names for the nomads' plants and animals.

This book inevitably favors the Bedouin male point of view. I was obliged to observe the strict sexual segregation Maʿaza tradition requires, so that other than in brief exchanges of greetings I had no access to the world and world view of Maʿaza women. Many of the male perspectives presented in this book may be shared by women, but others certainly are not. Women may possess a richer or different body of knowledge about the natural environment, an important focus of the book, than do men. Spending nearly all of their days pasturing sheep and goats, women may for example know much more about plants and their utility than men do. I hope that a woman will go into the field to develop a more complete record of Bedouin lifeways, by researching and describing the Eastern Desert of Maʿaza women.

Introduction

From the tabletop summit of the South Galala Plateau, we saw the plain of Wadi 'Araba, where we had begun walking at dawn, stretched out below us all the way from the Gulf of Suez to the Nile Valley. We soon lost this view in the plateau's labyrinthine canyonland. Saalih 'Ali paused frequently, for he had the difficult task of navigating this terrain. Muhammad Umbaarak walked confidently just ahead of us, setting our pace. Although in his early seventies, Muhammad walked with the ease and grace of a young man, and he took the whims of the Galala landscape in stride.

We stopped to rest in 'Adayd, one of the Galala's largest gorges. Saalih and Muhammad teased one another like boys, and I watched as Saalih dumped the contents of his friend's *sufun* out on the sand. This purse of ibex skin held everything that Muhammad considered essential for his everyday needs. Saalih itemized the contents: the steel striker, flint, and tindercloth that graybeards like Muhammad often use in place of matches; a book of matches; a knife; a signet ring bearing Muhammad's name and the Muslim year 1367 (A.D. 1941), used for those rare but inevitable government documents requiring a Bedouin's signature; the identity card that enabled him, like all Egyptians, to buy subsidized goods in government cooperatives; a seashell to be applied to the skin in the event of a scorpion sting; antimony powder for an eye infection; a gazelle horn used to store this powder and the dipstick for applying it; an aspirin; some wire; a pencil; cash; tweezers, for adding and removing glowing coals from his tobacco pipe; and the pipe. Muhammad had forged the bowl of his pipe from a piece of an Israeli aircraft that had crashed during one of the wars with Egypt. He had carved its stem from the wood of the wild fig tree.

"Men who dwell in the country are better than men who dwell in the city," wrote Ibn Khaldun in the fourteenth century, "for the former seek only the necessities of life from the soil not the superfluities and thus do not give their hearts to material things. Men who dwell on the land have a strong feeling for the common good and only those who have this feeling can dwell on the land" (Father Kevin Wall, personal communication).

This book is about a people who live unencumbered by material posses-sions, bound by kinship and livelihood to a desert wilderness of sand and rock. Their home is eastern Egypt, between the Nile River and the Red Sea. Their tribe is the Maʿaza, the "Goat People." Their clan, a subunit of the tribe, is the Khushmaan, the "Nose People": all clan members living today are descended from a common male ancestor of twelve generations ago whose name was al-Khasham, "the Nose." The Khushmaan are pas-toral nomads: pastoral in that they raise sheep, goats, and camels; nomadic in that they move these animals to wherever rain has fallen and pasture sprouted in the vast Eastern Desert. They have no fixed dwellings: home is a mobile woolen tent or a temporary windscreen of dead plants.

This book is a portrait of Bedouin life. The emphasis is on how the Bed-ouins themselves view their world. Remarkably, this approach is widely discouraged in modern scholarship on pastoral nomadism. The anthropol-ogist Emanuel Marx, for example, complains that some of the classical writers about nomadism were content with reporting what the Bedouins told them about Bedouin society and that even the most acute observers emphasized those aspects of society that the Bedouins themselves regarded as the most important (E. Marx 1978, 42). Emphasizing what the Bedouins believe to be important is precisely the object of this book. As a geog-rapher trained in the humanistic tradition, I am convinced that the beliefs, attitudes, and perceptions of a society profoundly influence the ways in which that society uses resources. In turn, the landscape with its associ-ations of plants, animals, and people reflects the values of that society. Therefore, there is no more important subject of study than what mem-bers of the society believe is most important.

A principal goal of this book is to record some of the raw material of Bedouin imagination and experience. This purpose is also disavowed by some scholars, including Neville Dyson-Hudson, who dislikes the "Sears Roebuck" tradition of Harold Dickson and other "able but incidental" ob-servers who painstakingly cataloged details of everyday activities and be-liefs of pastoral nomads. At the same time, Dyson-Hudson laments the "simple if somewhat gloomy truth" that extraordinarily little is known about human behavior in nomadic societies and insists that, in order to break free of old, unsatisfactory generalizations about nomadism, much more information must be acquired about specific situations in nomadic life (Dyson-Hudson 1972, 5, 21). Marx reminds us that in the classical litera-ture on nomadism—including, apparently, the "Sears Roebuck" works—there remains a great deal of raw information that modern scholars have not exploited adequately. "The common belief that our knowledge about the Bedouin is extensive and that we understand their society better than other sectors of the population of the Middle East is unfounded," he con-cludes (E. Marx 1978, 43). It is hoped that this book will increase knowledge about a particular group of nomads whose insights would otherwise go unrecorded and, more generally, about a way of life that is disappearing all the way from Morocco to India.

Perhaps this book will also promote understanding. One reason for the retreat of pastoral nomadism is that nonnomads do not understand how Bedouins live and view life. This ignorance is a source of fear and repression. Rather than try to change the nomads, sedentary powers-that-be might, with more understanding about the desert people, benefit from the detailed knowledge and extraordinary skills that Bedouins have acquired through ages of habitation and experience in the wilderness.

Bedouin Life
in the Egyptian Wilderness

1. The Desert and Its People

The Ma'aza Bedouins occupy a small portion of a vast arc of arid landscapes spanning northern Africa and southwestern Asia. This is the world's largest expanse of dry lands, in which the overall mean annual precipitation is less than twelve inches (300 mm) (Krader 1959, 501). Cultivation of grain on a regular basis requires a minimum mean annual precipitation of ten–twelve inches (250–300 mm), and thus an agricultural way of life is impossible in all but a few anomalous habitats within this arid region (E. Marx 1978, 47). This huge void has been filled by the world's most accomplished and numerous nonagriculturalists and nonurbanites, the pastoral nomads.

Any discussion of pastoral nomads inevitably concerns the interaction of physical geography and social patterns. So direct is the correlation between nomads and nature that pastoral nomadism is frequently defined by this association; Douglas Johnson, for example, identifies this way of life as a "rational response to a moisture-deficient, fragile environment" (1973, 3). Certainly Ma'aza life cannot be appreciated without attention to the physical and social characteristics of the Ma'aza landscape and to the ways in which these features reflect one another.

Physical Environment

The Ma'aza Bedouins live in the northern half of Egypt's Eastern Desert, named for its location east of the Nile River. The western and eastern boundaries of Ma'aza territory are, respectively, the Nile floodplain and the body of water comprising the Gulf of Suez and the Red Sea. The northern boundary is the plain cut by Wadi 'Araba. The southern boundary is the asphalt road linking the town of Qift in the Nile Valley to Qoseir on the Red Sea coast. The respective latitudes are, roughly, 29°N and 26°N, equivalent to the situation of southern Texas between San Antonio and the Mexico border or to northern India between Delhi and Varanasi. The total area is approximately fifty-six thousand square miles (90,000 sq.

km), slightly smaller than the state of Indiana or the nation of Portugal, and composes 8.5 percent of Egypt's total land area.

In the interior of this vast area (excluding towns of the Red Sea coast and Nile Valley), the number of human inhabitants—composed exclusively of nomadic Bedouins—is probably no more than one thousand, or about one person per fifty-six square miles (90 sq. km). This is one of the lowest population densities on earth, a fact that can be appreciated by looking at what this land offers, or fails to offer: it is an exceptionally difficult area in which to live.

To begin with, the land is rugged. There is considerable geologic and topographic complexity in Ma'aza country, with igneous, sedimentary, and metamorphic rocks present. A line starting at the Red Sea coast and running through the heart of Khushmaan territory to the Nile Valley first crosses a barren coastal plain spanning about thirty miles (45 km) from the shoreline to the base of a great mountain range of igneous and metamorphic rock. The highest mountains (up to 7,175 ft., 2,187 m) erupt suddenly from this plain. A gentle mix of granitic and metamorphic foothills follows, giving way to the forty-mile-wide (65 km) plain of Wadi Qena. On the western side of this plain, a limestone wall rises, and beyond it lies a vast plateau up to 2,840 feet (865 m) high, cut by innumerable watercourses. This plateau ends in a high overlook of the Nile Valley.

The climate is harsh. Summers are hot and dry, and winters mild and dry. Winter nights can be very cold, particularly, the Bedouins note, during forty days corresponding to a Coptic fast. This is when clouds of the type the nomads call *arwayii* hang on mountain summits, portending not rain but intense cold. Frost touches the Red Sea coastal plain in these days. Even snow is known. On a warm mid-February night in southern Ma'aza territory, we were visited by a nomad who had just come from the region of Jebel Ghaarib, 135 miles (220 km) to the north. He described "white water," apparently snow, clinging to the higher portions of this 5,745-foot (1,751 m) mountain a week earlier. In 1984 a knee-deep snowfall on the South Galala Plateau lingered for six days. More notably, for it occurred farther south, on 6 January 1886 an overnight snowfall whitened shrubs in Wadi Umm Diisa and made Jebel Shaayib, the region's highest mountain, "look like the Matterhorn" (Floyer 1887, 678). Winter (*ash-shitta*) gives way to the nomads' favorite season, spring (*ar-rabii'a*), when leaves reappear on wild figs and other deciduous trees. Annual vegetation prompted by winter moisture explodes into green; satiated livestock bear young; and people drink milk. This time of cool nights and pleasant, cloudless days soon falls to the hot, dry summer (*as-sayf*), when people limit their activities to the early morning and late afternoon and spend long hours, like their livestock, in the shade of rock overhangs. Very high temperatures have been recorded. There was an extraordinary heat wave between 6 and

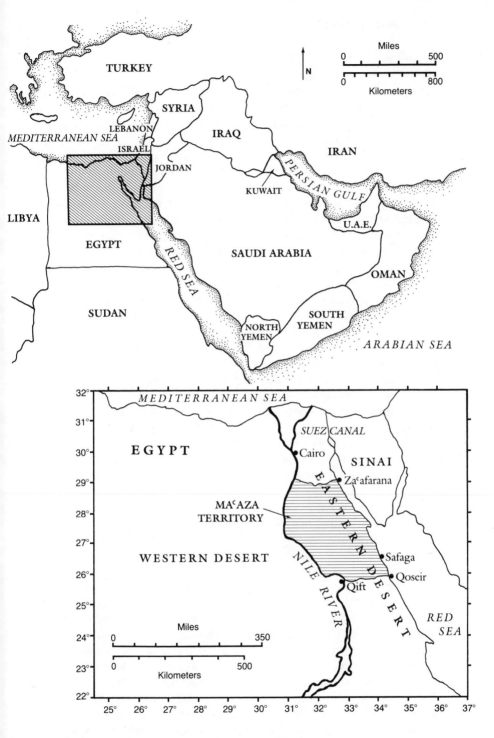

Map 1. Relative Location of the Maʿaza Territory

16 June 1886, when, even at night, the thermometer did not drop below 114°F (45.6°C) (Floyer 1887, 672). The stifling heat of summer is relieved by the shortening days of autumn (*al-khariif*) and finally broken by the "rainy days" (*an-naww*) of late October through December. These are times for anticipating more than enjoying rain, as cloud masses typically come and go without producing.

Bedouin life is focused on the high mountains and the wadis (watercourses) draining them, for this is the topography that "makes" rain. In winter the Red Sea mountains wring moisture out of low-pressure weather systems that swing down from the Mediterranean Sea. In summer the mountains sometimes generate convective rainfall, producing intense, short-lived thunderstorms and dramatic lightning shows that the nomads call "scorpions" (*ʿagrabaan*) for their resemblance to the fierce, spindly arachnids. Bedouin moods and behavior change dramatically in anticipation of "Mercy from God," as they call rain, and the flood (*sayl*) which may occur. The nomads move their livestock and belongings to higher ground, seeking or excavating dry shelters in which to wait out the potential deluge. Very dramatic rainfall episodes can occur. In 1954 rain fell heavily over much of the western portion of Maʿaza territory, swelling the normally dry, 185-mile (300 km) Wadi Qena. The rampaging waters caused widespread damage in the Nile Valley city of Qena, located at the wadi's mouth (Kassas and Girgis 1964, 61).

Such dramas in the desert are unusual, for precipitation is famously unreliable. Not only is total rainfall very low statistically, measuring, for example, only .12 inches (3 mm) annually at the Red Sea town of Hurghada, but rain falls willy-nilly at unpredictable times and locations (Kassas and Zahran, 1965, 157). It may pour heavily over a very small area and completely spare adjacent districts for years and even decades.[1] Even great rainfall events seldom last more than one or two hours; "It does not rain for seven or eight hours," one Bedouin stated flatly after I asked him, "What happens when . . ." During the fifteen months between November 1982 and February 1984, I actually saw rain only once, and that was a mere trace. However, I also visited the northern escarpment of the South Galala Plateau about a week after a torrential cloudburst and saw the effects, legendary among the Bedouins, of a flash flood: dry basins transformed to brimming pools and sandy watercourses scoured clean of dead vegetation and filled in with green seedlings. Months later I saw the nomads' dreamscape, a former wasteland laced with green and flowering watercourses.[2]

This phenomenon of brief, localized rainfall, followed by profuse but spotty and short-lived plant growth, provides the basis for Bedouin life. People and their domestic animals are creatures physically unfit to withstand drought conditions. Pastoral nomadism is simply a method for people and herds to avoid drought by migrating to wherever water and

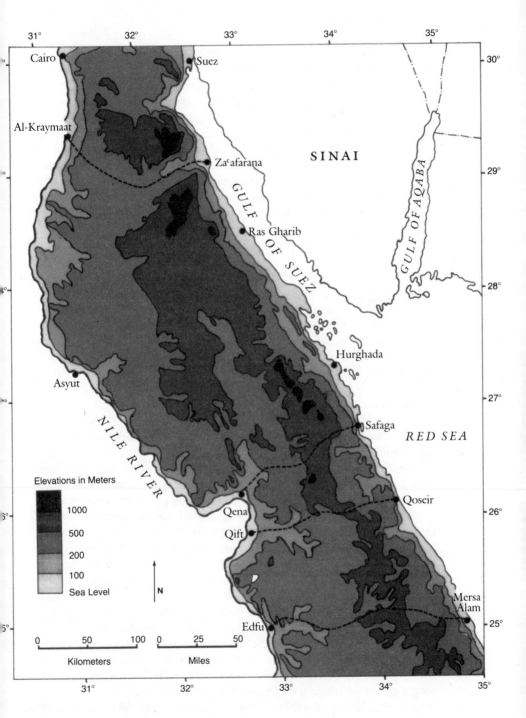

Map 2. Topography of the Northern Eastern Desert

pasture are available. In their livelihood the nomads replicate nature; their herd animals are domestic counterparts of wild creatures which survive by migrating. Sheep, goats, camels, and their wild equivalents feed on plants that evade drought in a different manner, by growing only when and where rain falls, and only for a limited time; most complete their life cycle within a year.[3]

Some desert plants and animals endure rather than avoid drought. These species are exceptionally resilient, surviving on scant available moisture. Among drought-enduring plants are the perennials such as acacia trees which tap permanent water sources deep underground.[4] While their livelihood is based primarily on avoiding drought, the Khushmaan nomads have also developed an extraordinary means of enduring drought by carefully exploiting their perennial trees, a practice described in detail in chapter 7.

Social Patterns

The nomads' adaptations of avoiding and enduring drought are successful because a set of social patterns and practices has evolved with these adaptations over thousands of years. Some of these social features are shared by all pastoral nomads. Others are common to most of the Arabic-speaking Bedouins of northeast Africa and southwest Asia and are well known from the literature on nomadism. These general features of Bedouin society merit discussion again here, along with the particulars of Khushmaan society, because they provide background information and vocabulary for the balance of this text.

The Ma'aza Bedouins perceive their desert as the "center of the universe." This improbable sense of security in the wilderness is largely a result of the social solidarity and practical benefits provided by the nomads' kinship system. The Ma'aza, like most Middle Eastern pastoral nomads, identify themselves by the patrilineal descent system: both men and women carry their father's name as surname and trace their genealogies exclusively through their fathers' fathers, all the way back to the man whom all members of the tribe recognize as their progenitor.[5] As they trace their ancestors back to the founder of the tribe, individuals recognize several, increasingly inclusive sets of the progenitor's patrilineal descendants: from the household to the lineage, clan, and finally tribe.

The tribe (*gabiila*) is the largest kinship unit the Bedouins acknowledge. Its membership represents the boundaries of a "chosen people"; non-tribesmen are strangers and outsiders whom, according to Bedouin ideology, can never become members of the tribe because their fathers were not. In actuality every tribe probably includes some people who were genealogically ineligible but who "became" members through peculiar circumstances. All Ma'aza tribesmen claim, however, to be patrilineal descendants of one man, Ma'iiz ibn al-Jabal ("Goat, Son of the Mountain"), who lived "long ago" in northwestern Arabia. His name reflects the environment and livelihood of his people, for the rugged mountain region of Midian in Arabia is the Ma'aza homeland. Here goats are the preferred domestic stock, and ibex, or wild goats, are the favorite game. The Scottish cartographer George W. Murray recorded one version of the tribe's origins in which the progenitor's wet-nurse was a goat; the founder and his brother were thus Arabian prototypes of Romulus and Remus (1950, 267). Whatever its origin, Ma'aza means "Goat People," and the goat is in effect the totem of this tribe.

The Ma'aza tribe comprises about twenty clans ('ayla), including the Khushmaan. All members of some Ma'aza clans have settled in the Nile Valley. However, some clans have populations in both the Nile Valley and the Eastern Desert; these are the Hamadiyiin, Tababna, Umsayri, Suwarha, Shuhbaan, Shaami, Muwaadhiya, Duwaasha, and Khushmaan. The Khushmaan have by far the most numerous and proportionately greatest number of desert-dwelling clan members, with about 125 households, or nine hundred people in the desert and an equal number in the Nile Valley. Desert-dwelling members of all other clans together probably comprise no more than one hundred persons.

The clan is a truer patrilineal kinship group than the tribe is. If you ask a Khushmaan man about his genealogy he will, without the benefit of charts, recite ten to fourteen generations through the male line. The genealogies of all Khushmaan lead to one common male ancestor. To be Khushmaan means, simply, to trace one's paternal grandfathers to this man, whose name was Mish'al. According to Khushmaan informants, the clan began in Arabia when Faayiz of the Jabaylaat clan and his son Mish'al distanced themselves from one another. Mish'al apparently had a disfigured nose; he was thus nicknamed "al-Khasham" ("the Nose") from which the clan takes its name. Mish'al begat 'Ayad; 'Ayad begat 'Awda; 'Awda begat Raashid; and Raashid begat Raadhi. Raadhi had two sons, 'Awaad and 'Iyd.

Khushmaan residence in Egypt began when Sulimaan, a son of 'Awaad, and Umbaarak, a son of 'Iyd, brought their families to the central Eastern Desert. That was five generations, or about 125 years, ago. All of the Egyptian Khushmaan trace their descent from Umbaarak, son of 'Iyd; Sulimaan, son of 'Awaad; and Sulaym, another son of 'Awaad who did not move to Egypt. These three were the progenitors of the local patrilineal descent groups, or lineages, that include all the Egyptian Khushmaan. Each lineage (called 'Ayaal n, after its founder) consists of many households (bayt, pl. buyuut).

Because the patrilineal system includes increasingly large segments of people descended from a common ancestor, it is known in studies of nomadism as the "segmentary lineage system." Scholars of nomadic cultures agree that the patrilineal descent system has a far greater importance in Bedouin life than merely designating a person's identity. These scholars are concerned especially with the relationship between kinship segments and the economic activities of pastoral nomads. They view memberships in household, lineage, clan, and tribe as prescriptions for specific social, economic, and political activities. In particular, they regard the segmented kinship structure as a cultural mechanism that allows people to disperse or congregate as the environmental conditions of drought or plenty warrant:

> Because the adaptive processes involved in animal husbandry require balances between stock, personnel to manage them, other forms of assets, and deployment to pastures or stubble fields, families cannot maximize the required balances without cooperation. The internal structure of the tribe—both in terms of residential groups, such as families, herding units, camps and camp groups, and the principles of social organization which define membership in lineages, "clans," and sections—is an accommodation to the exigencies of nomadism.
> (W. Swidler 1973, 30)[6]

Patterns in the everyday activities of the Khushmaan Maʿaza justify these academic conclusions about environment and nomadic culture. Every aspect of Khushmaan life is in some way tied to segmentary social organization. Kinship is involved in making a living, as common members of patrilineal descent groups congregate and disperse into camping parties to keep up with the changing availability of water and pasture. Cooperation between households of the same lineage or clan forms the basis for most economic and social activities. Flexible social and economic arrangements between members of household, lineage, and clan allow the nomads to exploit a wide range of opportunities more efficiently. Men leave the household to work, hunt, harvest, or shop; women move the camp and tend livestock; children supervise the animals. A single household often does not have enough members to perform all the tasks necessary to sustain itself, particularly during drought. Practical and aesthetic benefits often bring two or more households together. A common pattern of encampment is for two or three *bayt*s from the same clan, and usually from the same lineage, to unite. Having several households together frees at least one male household head to be absent for long periods to work for wages, collect wild plants, hunt, or travel to town to shop, while one or more older males remain in camp.

Scholars of nomadism are, at the same time, correct in noting that segmentation in practice is more flexible than the rote genealogies of the Bedouins themselves would suggest; "in real life the units do not necessarily amalgamate according to the genealogical scheme; the amalgamation proceeds always according to the governing interest of the particular moment" (E. Marx 1978, 60).[7] The Khushmaan, for example, sometimes camp with the ʿAbabda tribe, members of a foreign tribal "nation," but people who provide at least temporarily the same kind of support that fellow kinspeople might. Thus it is the built-in flexibility of the segmentary lineage system, rather than the rigid categories of membership officially designated by that system, that represents a successful cultural adaptation to desert conditions.

While the Khushmaan may affiliate themselves temporarily with people of other clans or even tribes, there is no substitute for the genuine emotion a person feels for his or her more immediate kin. The strength of these bonds shows in the touching moments of a desert greeting, in the boyish tricks men play on one another, and in the hospitality for which Bedouins are famous the world over. When two persons meet they join in a handshake and, if they are kin or friends, a series of kisses on either cheek, all the while exchanging the greeting *salamaat!* ("salutations!"). The more intimate their association, the longer the exchange; sometimes it lasts for minutes. When man and woman meet, even husband and wife or mother and son, the man extends his right hand for the woman to kiss lightly two or three times. Then comes a series of questions about family: how is so-and-so? The person being called on prepares tea as soon as possible, followed by a meal if the visitor is not hurried. Farewells typically are subdued versions of hellos, with a plea to extend best wishes to all the relatives, "every one, from the biggest right down to the smallest."

Marriage in Khushmaan society, as in most pastoral nomadic cultures of the Middle East, reflects a compelling desire to maintain the integrity of membership in the patrilineal descent system. Marriages are arranged by the spouses' families and, with few exceptions, unite members of the Maʿaza tribe. A Tababna clanswoman once married outside the tribe to an Egyptian man, and a new clan, the Umsayri ("the Egyptian"), was established to legitimize this anomaly. Most marriages unite a man and woman from the same clan, and most of these unions are within a lineage. The ideal marriage, as in most Muslim Middle Eastern societies, is that of a man to his *bint ʿamm* (father's brother's daughter). If such a marriage is impossible, the next best is to the other first cousin, *bint khall* (the mother's brother's daughter). There are few enough of these ideal partnerships that consequences of inbreeding are not widespread in the Khushmaan population, although in one lineage I did observe a high incidence of deafness and lack of speech.

The age of first marriage is generally twenty to twenty-five for men and seventeen to twenty for women. Subhi ʿAwaad and Dakhilallah Saliim are renowned for having waited until they were about thirty-five to marry for the first time. "You don't want to marry a girl over twenty-two," Saalih admonished me; "she's mostly finished by thirty." A woman has an average of six children. By divorcing and/or having multiple wives, some men foster prodigious families. ʿAwaad Saliim had seven wives and a total of nineteen children (Tregenza 1958, 90). In 1986, at the age of about seventy-five, Sulimaan Maraʿi was looking for a woman of childbearing age. His present wife was near fifty and could not deliver. He had been searching for at least four years with no luck, as prospective fathers-in-law were reluctant to give a daughter away to such an old man.

The groom pays a dowry of $625–$750 (500–600 £E), the equivalent of one camel. The Egyptian Maʿaza are not wealthy, and this represents a considerable expense. "Back in the 1920s, when my father married," Saalih mused, "the dowry was only $6.25" (5 £E). If the would-be bride's father is reluctant to give his daughter away, the contract can often still be made, but for a heavy price of up to five camels. The Arabian Maʿaza pay a standard dowry equivalent to $2,500 (2,000 £E). Egyptian brides are thus bargains for Arabian grooms; Muhammad Umbaarak and others have given daughters away to Saudi Maʿaza grooms. However, would-be Egyptian Maʿaza consorts of Arabian women cannot afford the bride-price.

The bride moves to the groom's or groom's father's camp to establish a new *bayt,* and both sets of parents present the newlyweds with several sheep, goats, and sometimes camels. One or more married sons often continue to live with their father (and mother, if they live together) to ensure that parents are secure later in life.

Polygamy is rare, even though Islam permits a man four wives if he treats them equally. In the early 1980s only four Khushmaan had more than one wife: one who lived in the Nile Valley with four, two in the desert with two, and Muhammad Umbaarak with three, two of whom lived together in the Nile Valley and a third, the youngest, who maintained Muhammad's principal *bayt* in the desert. The latter was clearly his favorite, for Muhammad visited his other wives only once or twice a year, and only for a few days.

Divorce is surprisingly common. The graybeard Umtayr Silmi had only one wife at the time of his death in 1984, but had divorced three. Divorced or widowed women rarely remain alone long if they are of childbearing age. A remarkable case was that of Jimayʿa, daughter of ʿAyd ʿIyd. First, ʿAwaad Saliim married her. They had three children before ʿAwaad died. Umtayr Silmi then married her, had a son by her, and divorced her. She finally married and bore a son to ʿAyd Musallim in his old age.

Khushmaan men take pride in their womenfolk, especially for their stamina. A woman spends almost her entire life outdoors, rarely making even the brief shopping trips to town that men do. Her presence in the wilderness with her children and the family herd represents the cornerstone of Bedouin identity as a desert people. Men often work in villages or towns for extended periods but return as often as possible to the desert household, and it is only when the woman and children leave the desert and settle in towns or villages that the family's Bedouin identity is lost. Once I helped Sulimaan Mara'i try to find his desert household after a long shopping trip to Hurghada. During his three-week absence, his wife, children, and livestock had relocated to new pasture, and we spent two days tracking them. We finally gave up, for they had gone too far north. I thought how strange it would be in our society for a man routinely not to know for several weeks where his wife, children, and "house" were. Sulimaan's son, Musallim, laughed about our adventure: "Our women are the best. They're not like city women, always asking where you're going and when you'll be back. You're free to roam when you leave them what they need." I wondered whether women praised their men in the same terms.

The Khushmaan are baffled and sometimes amused by kinship arrangements in other cultures. Not getting married is unimaginable to the Khushmaan. Saalih felt that the monks of St. Anthony's and St. Paul's monasteries were completely mad, living lives without wives and children, "a life worse than death." The Khushmaan are incredulous that under no circumstances may an 'Abadi man speak to his mother-in-law, "even if he is dying of thirst and could be saved by asking her for water." Saalih asked me whether we always married within our own clan. He was astonished when I explained that we had no clans and that anyone could marry anyone else. He roared with laughter when I told him that it was largely forbidden for us to marry our first cousins. 'Abd al-Dhaahir Sulimaan was no less surprised and amused when I told him that in India the dowry system was reversed, with women "purchasing" husbands.

2. Nomads and Neighbors

Anthropologists have argued that the segmentary lineage organization is particularly important for nomads' survival because nomads lack stable territorial boundaries in which to practice their livelihood (e.g., Salzman 1978, 627, 628). In this view the nomads' lack of a homeland, with all the economic and ideological deficiencies this shortcoming implies, is compensated for by strong social cohesion.

Ma'aza and Khushmaan experience suggests that scholars of nomadism have placed too little emphasis on the importance of territory and homeland in Bedouin life. The Ma'aza tribe and the Khushmaan and other clans have carved out for themselves large and jealously guarded territories which, as much as kinship segments, play important roles in everyday economic activities.

The nomads' territorial interests are not matters that concern only the Bedouins. Ma'aza and Khushmaan fulfillment of "manifest destiny" in the desert has had wide-ranging impacts on other nomadic groups and on nonnomads in Egypt. Conflicts over territories in the desert interior and larger-scale confrontations between the people of two natural regions, the desert and the Nile oasis, have been instrumental in forming the unique identities of the nomads' kinship segments and have shaped lingering perceptions which set the nomads apart from their neighbors.

Establishment of the Egyptian Homeland

The Ma'aza of Egypt have their origins in the Arabian Peninsula, where the Ma'aza are also known as the Bani 'Atiyya. There is no certain explanation of why and when they came to Egypt. What scant published information exists depicts all the nomads arriving in one migration. The Swiss explorer John Burckhardt related that 250 Ma'aza households left Arabia for Egypt on the same date, apparently in the 1700s, after a defeat by their raiding enemies the Howeitat. Some traveled to Egypt by sea. Many who attempted the trip overland were killed by the Howeitat (quoted in Murray 1950, 267 n. 2). This sounds suspiciously like a Howeitat version of events. The Ma'aza rendition is that the Arabian Ma'aza had contact as visitors to the Eastern Desert long before it became a homeland. Over a long period of time, both defeat at home and opportunity abroad brought them to the new land.

In Arabia, raiding had long been an important adjunct to the pastoral economy. The typical pattern was a brief sortie by members of one tribe on the camp of another. Camels or other livestock and furnishings were the usual booty taken. A retaliatory raid followed. So regular and even was this exchange that some social Darwinists view raiding as an unintentional cultural mechanism to maintain a long-term ecological balance between herds, pasture, and people (e.g., Sweet 1965).

To the mobile Ma'aza, Nile Valley settlements and major caravan and pilgrim routes across the Eastern Desert were inviting targets. Ma'aza raiders took advantage of these opportunities, riding from Arabia through the Sinai, often skirmishing along the way with traditional enemies including the Howeitat, Terabiin, Tiyaaha, and Billi, who sometimes pursued them far into Egypt. The Ma'aza found Nile Valley peasants to be easy prey. Their favorite tactic was to steal and ransom farmers' livestock. On long, moonless winter nights, the raiders would cut loose a few cattle, load them with clover, and head into the desert. Then they would send in a delegate demanding ransom of about half of each animal's worth. Farmers usually paid up; otherwise, their animals were killed or driven up the "Thieves' Road" to market (Russell 1949, 56–57).

The Ma'aza also preyed on caravans in the Eastern Desert, where they made enemies of the indigenous nomadic 'Ababda tribesmen, for the caravan routes lay in 'Ababda territory and were under 'Ababda protection. A milestone in the early days of Ma'aza-'Ababda conflict was the 'Ababda killing of Ruwayshid, a Ma'aza leader of the Qisisat clan. Ruwayshid was a desert general, a commander ('aqiid) of raiding parties, a strapping man with a mustache so long he tied it behind his ears. The 'Ababda version of events is that Ruwayshid's wife commanded him to bring her the head of an 'Abadi so she could admire the famed 'Ababda coiffure. Ruwayshid said he would. While scouting for victims, Ruwayshid himself fell to an 'Ababda spear and was buried in Wadi al-Ghuzaa in a Nabatean tomb (Murray 1950, 268; Wilkinson 1832, 52). The burial site was at an acacia under which Ruwayshid had had an apparent premonition, for before setting out that fateful day he had asked his companions to bury him there.

The killing set off a blood feud. In a wadi not far from where Ruwayshid died, his kinsman 'Agiil built a cairn to attract curious 'Ababda and concealed himself nearby to ambush and kill any takers. Two graves today attest to the success of his ploy. An 'Ababda raiding party soon plundered a Ma'aza caravan, and in retaliation a large group of Ma'aza ambushed and killed forty 'Ababda at a place called Mawgif al-Khalfaat.

By the late eighteenth century, the Ma'aza presence in the Eastern Desert was greater than ever before. Raiders stayed on to fight the ʿAbabda and loot caravans, rather than return to Arabia. Maʿaza tribesmen who escorted desert caravans eventually settled along the Nile Valley. By about 1805, after decades of both peaceful trading and bloody hostilities, the Maʿaza won a tribal territory in the Eastern Desert, extending as it still does from Wadi ʿAraba to the Qift-Qoseir road.

Maʿaza oral history and government records offer conflicting versions of an important event preceding agreement over Maʿaza boundaries. Both accounts concur that a Maʿaza raiding party attacked a caravan traveling from Qift, in the Nile valley, to Qoseir, on the Red Sea coast. The raiders seized the *kiswa* (the broadcloth made in Cairo to cover the Kaʿaba of Mecca, Islam's holiest shrine). In 1803, according to government sources, the Egyptian ruler Muhammad ʿAli retaliated for this sacrilege:

> A caravan from the mountains in Upper Egypt arrived at the capital with a lot of camels and goods, belonging to the Maʿaza Arabs, for trading, as is the custom of caravans. When this news reached Muhammad ʿAli, he at once got up at night, and while men were asleep he suddenly attacked the caravan with his men, pillaging their camels, loads, and goods, even the sons, women, and daughters, and led them as prisoners inside the city. Then he started to sell them as he had previously done with the natives of Kafr Hakim and its neighbourhood. (Quoted in Murray 1950, 268)

Maʿaza Bedouins told me that their ancestors did capture the broadcloth, but denied that the government took punitive action. Rather, Cairo sought accommodation. Saalih related the following version when we visited Wadi Gush, site of the notorious raid. The wadi's name means "offal," referring to the remains of the men killed there. Saalih spoke as we stood on what he said was the common grave of four hundred government soldiers who had been escorting the caravan:

> They were peasant-soldiers, Egyptians working for the Turks. They were five hundred. The Maʿaza party numbered between seventy and eighty. During the skirmish, four hundred soldiers died, but not a single Maʿaza. The soldiers would fire more or less rapidly, according to the beat of a drum. They had a superior rifle called a *bruusi,* while the Maʿaza had their flintlocks [*fatiila*]. The raiders had an advantage, though: they were in small parties on the ridges on each side of the wadi [which is about 250 ft., or 75 m wide]. The Maʿaza did not bury the government's dead. They retired to the mountain of Umsikat al-Juukh [Mount "Seizure of the Broadcloth"] and divided the booty, before heading for the Galaala.

Land was given to the Maʿaza after this, so that no more raiding would occur. What happened was this: a week before the raid on the

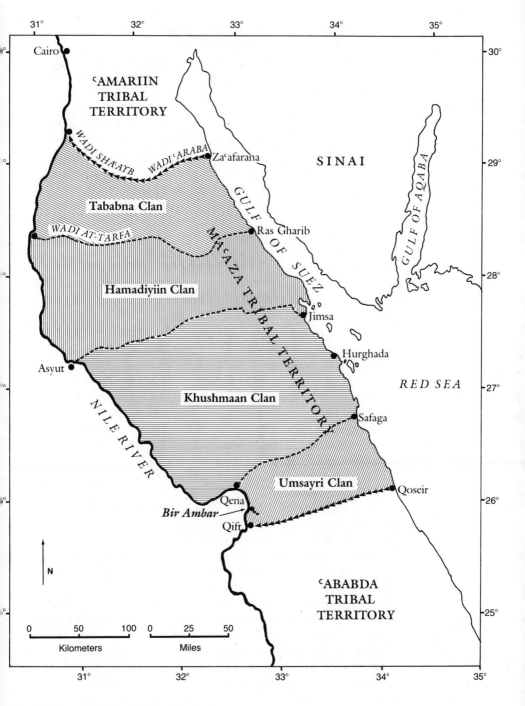

Map 3. Maᶜaza Tribal and Clan Territories

caravan, a delegate representing the Maʿaza arrived at the palace of "the pasha" [apparently, Muhammad ʿAli] in Cairo. He carried ten meters of white cloth and a kid goat tied on a rope. He greeted the pasha and saw him surrounded by guards. The pasha asked him, "Why do you have the goat and the cloth?" The Maʿazi replied, "You may kill me. Here is the cloth you will lay me in, and here the kid you will slaughter at my grave." The pasha replied, "You will not die. But why do your people always raid?" The Maʿazi responded, "We are hungry, and have no land, as your government has claimed all of it." The pasha said, "I will give you land if you will not raid." The Maʿazi agreed to consider this, arranged a return date to see the pasha, and left.

Ten minutes later the Maʿazi returned. The pasha asked, "What, you don't want the armistice?" The Maʿazi, not wanting to appear to go back on his word, told the pasha: "I have heard that our great raider Haamid al-Ashram ["The Hairlip"] is headed for the Qift-Qoseir caravan road. What will happen to our agreement if he makes a raid there?" The pasha answered, "If our forces under Mahmuud Pasha destroy your men, so be it; if your forces under Haamid al-Ashram destroy ours, so be it; there will still be peace."

Soon, the news reached the pasha that his forces had been routed and the caravan pillaged. The Maʿaza delegate arrived to keep his appointment, and the pasha asked him for a meeting with Haamid al-Ashram. Later, the pasha received al-Ashram in the Citadel of Cairo. To test him, the pasha had twenty pottery jugs set up. He had his best marksmen fire. They struck a few targets, but most of their bullets missed. Then it was al-Ashram's turn. His flintlock was built to fire two shots in succession. While firing, al-Ashram ran back and forth parallel to the line of jugs. In two minutes he knocked off twenty jugs. The pasha called to the Maʿaza delegate, "Get hold of your wild man! Get hold of your wild man!"

Then the pasha asked al-Ashram, "Where are your forces and strength?" Al-Ashram responded, "In the west, from Wadi Shaʿayb to Bir Ambar, and in the east, from Zaʿafarana to Qoseir." The pasha granted these as the boundaries of Maʿaza territory and invested Haamid al-Ashram at Bani Mazar as the first Maʿaza headman [ʿumda] in Egypt.

The Maʿaza regarded themselves as a tribal nation which fought for and won a homeland in Egypt. The ʿAbabda saw Maʿaza acquisition of territory as Cairo's compromise with a ruthless and undeserving invader. In the government view, the treaty boundary between warring ʿAbabda and Maʿaza tribes was a sensible political settlement of a volatile situation in a strategically important area.

Kushmaan oral history suggests that it is misleading to focus on how "the Ma'aza" settled their new homeland. It was not an entire tribe that migrated. Rather, a few households from some clans began settling in Egypt in the eighteenth century. The Khushmaan households were among the last to emigrate, and many clanmembers remained in Arabia. Sulimaan 'Awaad Raadhi in about 1885 established the first Khushmaan household in Egypt. The last immigrants were 'Awda Sulimaan and 'Ayd Musallim, who left Arabia after World War I (they had seen trains recently blown up by T. E. Lawrence "of Arabia" and his Bedouin guerrillas). 'Ayd outlived 'Awda and died in 1985.

The Khushmaan speak of the warfare that drove them out of Arabia but emphasize the opportunities that attracted them to Egypt:

> In Arabia the acacias and other trees had been cut. The ibex had all been hunted, and there was little pasture. In Egypt, there was water in the interior. The mountains were full of ibex. We used to come from Arabia to buy grain and other supplies in Qena. We made acacia charcoal to sell in the Nile Valley and bought provisions there. People returned to Arabia saying, "Egypt is rich." So, we started coming. In Arabia there was always warfare, raiding, and killing. Raiders came from as far away as Syria to attack us. In Egypt there was peace.

'Ayd Musallim elaborated on how he and his predecessors came to know Egypt. Juhayna tribesmen from Arabia piloted ships between the Arabian and Egyptian shores of the Red Sea, landing in Egypt at the now-defunct port of Guwayh between Safaga and Qoseir. Among their clients were Ma'aza, including Khushmaan, pastoralists from Arabia who annually ferried their produce of goat cheeses, ghee, palm fiber, and dates to Egypt. Other Ma'aza tribesmen who had preceded them from Arabia escorted them on camels across the Eastern Desert to the Nile Valley market of Qena. There, the traders exchanged their Arabian goods for millet, cloth, and sometimes goats. Then they returned to Arabia. The whole excursion lasted one month. 'Ayd visited Egypt once this way. On three other excursions, including his last, he was working with 'Igayl traders who brought five hundred to one thousand camels at a time out of Arabia, crossing the Sinai on foot and the Suez Canal on ferry to reach the camel market at Imbaba, near Cairo. 'Ayd finally stayed, marrying an Egyptian-born daughter of his kinsman Mara'i. Many family members, including his brothers Sulaym, Raashid, and Saalih, are still in Arabia, and the Egyptian and Saudi kin communicate by mail with the help of literate intermediaries. "When you go to Tobuk," 'Ayd told me, "you will find Sulaym by asking at the well of Bir Shigri. He will certainly slaughter a sheep for you!" 'Ayd explained that while Ma'aza raiding incursions into Egypt ended when the Suez Canal was built (1869), peaceful exchanges continued until the Saudi government restricted entry into the kingdom and the Saudi Khushmaan began enjoying oil wealth. Thereafter, there was little incentive for Saudi Khushmaan to visit Egyptian kin, except to acquire a bride. Saudi citizens can afford the expense to travel to Egypt and return with a wife, but Egyptian Khushmaan are too poor to reciprocate: boat service ceased about 1950, and the cost of air travel is prohibitive.

The Egyptian Khushmaan missed the classical days of raiding against Nile peasants and the ʿAbabda, but were involved in an inglorious conflict with a colonial power. The English and their Egyptian agents were formidable adversaries. The Khushmaan began fighting them only after the English claimed to have "pacified" the Eastern Desert. In 1885 a colonial explorer confidently wrote, "Public security is not dependent on the Bedawin since Baker Pasha and his police took up their duties in Upper Egypt" (Floyer 1887, 661). There was conflict, however, resulting largely from the salt monopoly the English imposed. As in India, once the colonial government granted an English company exclusive rights to the salt trade, any other mining or trading of salt, even for personal use, was illegal; such salt was contraband and its merchants were criminals (Russell 1949, 55). This policy created a lucrative opportunity for the Maʿaza, who lived on top of the Mallaaha salt flat, described as containing "sufficient salt for the whole world and the last important saline on the way to India" (Von Dumreicher 1931, 134). A period of bloodshed ensued. The English established a chain of Coastguard patrol stations to prevent salt "thefts." Under an English commander, each had a team of camel-mounted Sudanese officers, Bisharin trackers, ʿAbabda and even Maʿaza guides called "the Partisans" (*az-Zuharaat*). These forces were effective and sometimes ruthless. "A lot of people died for the salt trade," Saalih told me, "so that the government could have its monopoly."

Nowadays the Maʿaza admire the English legacy, represented by the foreigners' engineering feats and by fine memories of Leo Tregenza. But they have not forgiven the English for their iron fist, nor have they forgotten men who hunted and shot them like dogs. One of the enforcers was a black man named Morgan, described by his commander as an extraordinary lance-corporal, a six-foot-four Nubian "of the gorilla type and strength . . . like a wild animal when drunk . . . who had wonderful eyesight and was the best shot in the corps" (Von Dumreicher 1931, 132). This man is apparently the "Murjaan" remembered today in Khushmaan folklore:

A group of Maʿaza was returning from working salt at al-Mallaaha. Murjaan and an English captain were approaching them on their tracks. My grandfather ʿIyd was with them. His camel somehow sensed the pursuers and would not go as ʿIyd ordered him to and kept straying off the path. ʿIyd's companions told him, "Your camel is mad. Nothing is wrong." But ʿIyd began scouting and soon saw the head of

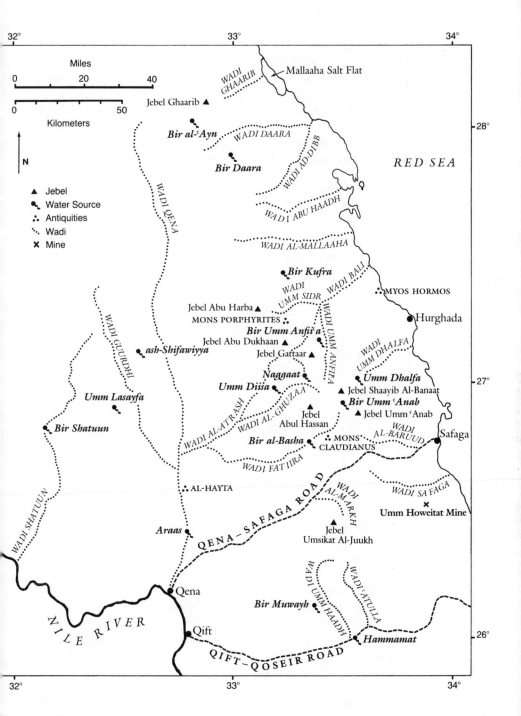

Map 4. Principal Locations Cited in the Text

a government man disappear behind a rock. The party dropped their load of salt, mounted their camels, and galloped away, except for a man named Farraj, who tried to flee on foot. From a distance Murjaan shot him in the shoulder. Farraj kept running until he reached this small rise here on the coastal plain. He covered his tracks and blood and buried himself in a rock crevice, covering it with stones. But Murjaan followed his tracks and eventually found Farraj, dead. This place is called Safra ibn Farraj ["Yellow Hill Place of Farraj"].

The English sensibly avoided involving Maʿaza trackers against Maʿaza "criminals." They did however employ ʿAbabda tribesmen against the Maʿaza, thus rekindling old hostilities between the two tribes. The Khushmaan today recite this account:

There was an ʿAbadi named Hussayn who was really despicable, always telling government people about the Maʿaza salt trade. Some Maʿaza finally caught up with him in Wadi al-Humraa, near Wadi al-Atrash. They told him, "You must die!" He boasted, "I lived like a man, I will die like a man." His captors replied, "All right, witness God so you can die." He was still defiant, "My wife in Qena is pregnant. And I will go in good time my own way!" His captors killed him on the spot. The place where he died, Kharam al-Hussayn, is named after him.

One of the last blood feuds between these tribes began when an ʿAbadi guide employed by the Coastguards helped track down and arrest a Maʿaza salt "thief." In retaliation some Maʿaza shot the tracker. The tracker's son then killed two Maʿaza, a father and son. In turn some Maʿaza killed two ʿAbabda. In 1908 the matter went to arbitration in a Nile Valley court, ironically administered by the English whose arbitrary law had sparked the incident (Russell 1949, 68–71). The authorities used blackmail: unless the Maʿaza ceased hostilities, ʿAbabda tribesmen would replace Maʿaza as custodians of the Qift-Qoseir caravan route (Von Dumreicher 1931, 137–138).

The salt monopoly ended in 1904. English intervention in desert affairs did not. In 1906 Thomas Russell, an inspector of interior, established the Police Camel Patrol. Its official responsibilities were to prevent hashish smuggling and illicit landings of Mecca pilgrims on the Red Sea coast. Russell decided that the patrol should also protect desert game. The Maʿaza respected his goal but despised his methods. Having forbidden hunting in the vast area of the Maʿaza Limestone Plateau bounded by the Nile Valley, Wadi Qena, and Wadi at-Tarfa, Russell and his deputies swept into Bedouin camps, arresting those who had hunted game for food and killing all pet dogs, for these might be used in hunting. While a proclaimed conservationist, Russell was an avid hunter. His quarry included Barbary sheep, then threatened and now extinct in the region. Russell boasted that by depriving ibex of water he was able to congregate fifty of these wild goats around a well at the former preserve of Prince Kamal el-Din in Wadi Rishrash. Some of the thirsty animals became his trophies (Russell 1949, 57, 117–122).

Nomad-Government Relations

Governments in the Middle East have traditionally feared Bedouins for their military capabilities. As early as 2325 B.C., the Pharaoh Pepi I directed a local governor to round up Eastern Desert nomads, and during Roman times the central government mobilized camel-mounted troops to do the same (Robinson 1935, 126). Scattered in small groups, the nomads were fast, mobile, and unpredictable; they were ideal guerrilla fighters. Sometimes the fear was well founded, for example, on the Turks' part when the British under Lawrence's command armed and directed Bedouin fighters against Ottoman interests in the Arabian Peninsula. While such fears linger, they are unreasonable in the present era of helicopter gunships and other technologies that nomads cannot outrun (e.g., Heathcote 1983, 147).

Nomads have always had to deal with provincial and national governments and have often benefited from formal relations with sedentary authorities. On the national level, the Ma'aza tribe is represented nominally by a headman (*ghaalib*) who resides in the Nile Valley at Bani Mazar, north of Minya. He has little real power. More authority rests on seven clan leaders (*shaykhs*) who live in several communities on the Red Sea coast and in the Nile Valley. There they answer and appeal to provincial officials in matters of security, services, and other issues that involve nomads with government. The *shaykh* plays a valuable role both for the officials who need someone to answer for the inscrutable and invisible nomads and for the Bedouins who consult him on problems associated with the settled world. The nomads also turn to their *shaykh* for social advice, entertainment, and environmental information during their periodic visits to town. The position is elected; clan males agree among themselves who is most suitable for the role. The current Khushmaan *shaykh* is a man who had already settled in one of the Red Sea towns because of poor health and whom his peers regard as shrewd and outgoing.

Ma'aza relations with governments are more amicable now than in the past. Like all Egyptians, the Bedouins are entitled to buy some goods at prices made very reasonable by heavy government subsidies. The nomads' most important monthly rations are flour (up to 220 lbs., or 100 kg, per family at a cost of $8.10, or 6.5 £E) and sugar (3.3 lbs., or 1.5 kg, per person at 55¢, or .45 P.T. [piasters]). To obtain these goods, the Bedouin must at the age of sixteen register for and be issued a permit. This *bataaga* bears his name, birthdate, and occupation (the nomad's card always lists "farmer") and specifies in what towns the card is valid. Ironically, even the nomad must deal with bureaucracy from the day he is born: a birth certificate is required to obtain a *bataaga*, so a father must travel to town to register his desert-born child.

Despite its benefits, the *bataaga* carries a price: it identifies the male Bedouin as an Egyptian citizen who, since the early 1960s, has been required to enter a three-year military service at the age of twenty. Almost everyone complies. Occasionally a defiant young man holds out in the desert, but typically is caught, fined, and jailed when he visits town and displays his *bataaga* in order to buy food.

In the army the nomads are introduced to a wide world in such places as Cairo and Alexandria. They return to the desert with a disdain for such places and for army life. The military has sometimes recognized the Bedouins' unequaled tracking skills and ordered the more fortunate recruits to fill their tours of duty as trackers in the division of border security. One Khushaymi elected to stay on as a tracker on the Mediterranean coast long after his mandatory service expired. During the 1973 war between Egypt and Israel, several Maʿaza were temporarily armed and posted at strategic water sources to fend off potential invaders.

During the Arab-Israeli conflicts of 1967–1973, the Egyptian army introduced a permanent scourge in the Maʿaza desert. Troops sowed land mines extensively along the Red Sea and Gulf of Suez coastlines and randomly around water sources and along paved and unsurfaced auto routes in the interior. The Bedouins know where the mines were originally laid; unfortunately, this information is often inadequate because flash floods move and rebury the explosives. Sweeping the mines is thus a difficult or even impossible proposition. The explosives have killed many camels, sheep, and goats. Fortunately, no Bedouins have died. Sulimaan Saalih escaped with only temporary hearing loss after treading on a mine near the Qena-Safaga road. Unwary outsiders have suffered more. An Egyptian student on a group tour of Mons Claudianus was killed at the well of Bir al-Basha in 1982, and Egyptian and foreign tourists have been injured and killed at a number of shoreline locations. The remains of two blown-up vehicles in Wadi ʿAraba tell an extraordinary story. In 1980 an employee of an oil company drove off the main road, apparently to steal some wire he had spotted. The wire was a broken-down boundary that marked a minefield. Unaware of this, the driver struck a mine and was killed. Several days later a Cairo taxicab driver spotted the vehicle and drove to it. Fully loaded with spare parts that he tore from the victim's car, his automobile struck a mine before reaching the safety of the road, and he was killed.

Overall, the army has a poor reputation among the nomads. "They are the enemies of freedom," one man said. "When you are on your way home in the mountains, soldiers stop you and ask you where you are going, what you are doing, what you want, and tell you it is forbidden to walk there."

Soldiers are also despised for killing Bedouin livestock and wild game indiscriminately and for chopping down trees for fuel. They represent only one of several non-Bedouin peoples the nomads dislike.

Bedouins and Barbarians

Nile-dwellers have always been more fearful than enchanted of the Egyptian desert. The ancient Egyptians classified their terrestrial world into good and bad lands: the benevolent "black land," named for the fecund black soil of the Nile Valley, and the unyielding "red land" of desert rock and sand. The sterile landscape south of the Nile's second cataract was the ancients' "Land of the Ghosts" (Weigall 1909, 173). "How evil is the way without water!" insists a fourteenth-century B.C. inscription in a temple of Seti I (Weigall 1909, 159). More recent travelers have had comparable impressions. Arthur Weigall, visiting Wadi al-Atrash in the heart of Khushmaan Ma'aza territory about 1910, recorded, "The scenery here is wild, desolate. . . . there was a feeling . . . that one was travelling on the moon" (1909, 99). His contemporary, Andre Von Dumreicher in nearby Wadi Qena, perceived a "sublime" panorama of "a wonderful lunar landscape, a lifeless and ageless world" (1931, 141).

Some outsiders have disliked not only the desert but its people. Weigall despised the Bedouins who escorted him in 1907: "There are no people in the world so slovenly, so unpractical . . . so *footling*, as the inhabitants of the Eastern Desert . . . ragged weaklings, of low intelligence and little dignity. . . . of all stupid people these unwashed miseries are the stupidest" (1909, 92–94). Sir Richard Burton, the great explorer of Africa, described the Ma'aza as "turbulent and dangerous; the men are professional robbers; and their treachery is uncontrolled by the Bedawi law of honour. They will eat bread and salt with the traveller whom they intend to murder" (quoted in Murray 1950, 267). In the Monastery of St. Anthony, which, although in the Eastern Desert, is surrounded by walls and populated by Nile-minded Copts, a monk complained to me of the "Bedouins and barbarians" who had troubled the settlement since its founding in the fourth century. The walls were there, he explained, because the nomads have always been "great thieves" who caused "much trouble." Three years later another monk there told me he had begged some local Bedouins not to take the life of a German explorer, Carlo Bergmann, who was traveling by camel through Wadi 'Araba.

Egyptian city-dwellers and rural folk are generally contemptuous of the desert and its inhabitants. Few Egyptians by choice spend a night in the desert. A popular novel, *The Road of Safety* by Sa'ad al-Din Wahba, satirizes the desperate self-saving efforts of intercity travelers whose bus has broken down on a desert road (Wahba 1967). It is a peculiar kind of disas-

ter scenario that the Western reader, who has some affinity with unpopu-
lated open space, cannot easily appreciate. To Egyptians, however, being
stranded in the desert is a nightmare; Wahba's work is black comedy.

The perceived threat of hostile Bedouins only adds to the bleak prospects for the unfortunate desert visitor. An Egyptian botanist, hoping to
do some collecting with a Bedouin guide in the Eastern Desert, solicited
my company: "There would be you and me, two of us against one Bedouin." I had difficulty obtaining a permit to travel in the Eastern Desert
because a well-meaning official in Cairo feared that Bedouins would kill
me. I was dismayed by the behavior of Egyptians whom I introduced to
my Bedouin companions during our visits to Hurghada. An Egyptian inn-
keeper there who was famous among foreign visitors and fellow townspeople for being kind and accommodating retreated into his house or
turned cold whenever my Bedouin companions called. Some words in col-
loquial Egyptian Arabic reveal the Nile-dwellers' attitudes. "Arab," that is,
"Bedouin," is a pejorative in the Nile Valley, meaning roughly "filthy
savage."[1]

Bedouin feelings about their settled neighbors in the Nile Valley are reciprocal. The nomads refer to all Nile Valley inhabitants, whether farmers
or townspeople, Egyptians or foreigners, as peasants (*fallaahiin*) and foreigners (*khawajaat*). The inability of nonnomads to cope with the desert is
a frequent subject of Bedouin ridicule. "They are donkeys; ask them which
way is up wadi and they will point down wadi." "There is a sure way to
identify a broken Egyptian camp. Egyptians sleep in the road, whether it's
a car or camel track." We visited an abandoned army camp in Wadi Qena,
examining artifacts characteristic of settled people: scrap metal, oil stains
on the sand, broken bottles and Cleopatra cigarette butts, magazine pho-
tos of movie stars pinned on the walls, and acacia limbs hacked up for firewood. Among the nomads' comments were, "Egyptians must be very
close to one other, like goats"; and "*fallaahiin* are like animals, except they
talk." One man said, "They are like goats except that they have mustaches
and no brains"; another retorted, "Maybe the life of goats is better than
theirs; goats don't get into big problems." In Wadi al-Baruud we saw
ongoing reconstruction of several low-lying buildings which had been destroyed by a flash flood. I asked my companions why people would rebuild
what would inevitably be destroyed again. "Their brains are like donkeys',"
said one; "Because they are like small goats," commented the other.

The Arabs are especially critical of how Nile Valley people sacrifice their
prime agricultural land to new construction because they fear living on the
desert edge:

> I've guided many Egyptians in the desert. They always want a bath
> and a rest, and lots of water. You could put an Egyptian in Wadi Qena
> with a jerrycan of water and warn him to use it carefully. He'd drink

half and spill the other half on the sand within three hours. When they take trips in the desert, it never occurs to them that they can stay at a different place each night. There's always a haul to get back to camp before dark. This wastes water. And they must have light all around them at night. They are stupid! Look at how they eat up their farming land with their towns like Qena, and look at how much land there is around them in the desert!

Musallim Sulimaan and Saalih had the kind of unfortunate experience that reinforces the Bedouins' dislike of "peasants." In 1967 they traveled to Cairo together for the first time to visit an ill kinsman. A few minutes after they hailed a cab near the Pyramids, the car pulled over, and four men climbed in. These new riders halted the taxi on an empty stretch of road. One pointed a rifle at the Bedouins and took all their money, $15 (12 £E). They ordered their victims to get out of the car and walk away without looking back, so they would not catch the license number of the cab, whose driver was presumably in cahoots with the thieves. In petty ways too, Egyptians regularly take advantage of them, claim the nomads. Settled people try to cheat them, believing they do not know the costs of given items and services.

The Khushmaan uphold certain values that, in their opinion, distinguish them from and make them superior to other peoples, even other Bedouins. They abhor unjust violence and thievery. They view the Mutayr, a seminomadic people of the Upper Egyptian Nile, as a tribe of murderous brigands. Mutayr tribesmen stole Khushmaan camels as recently as the 1940s. They murder their own relatives and way-fellows with whom they have eaten bread and salt, not sparing even women and children, claim the Khushmaan. Muhammad Umbaarak explained why he feared the Mutayr:

> Back in the 1940s, on the desert plateau above as-Saff, a man of the ʿAmariin tribe was traveling with a woman relative and her six-month-old child. Two Mutayr men arrived, and in customary fashion the ʿAmari man gave them tea and food and invited them to spend the night. When the host retired, the Mutayr stayed up, talking loudly. The ʿAmari man asked politely why they were so restless. They replied that they were cold and could not sleep. He gave them blankets. While he slept, his Mutayr guests crept up and struck him in the head with a heavy stick. Then they went to where the woman and baby were and shot both of them. The mother died immediately, her child a day and a half later. While the Mutayr were murdering the others, the man was dragging himself into thick vegetation on the wadi floor. The Mutayr came back to take his money and found him gone. In the darkness they were spooked and hurriedly packed up the man's possessions and fled without finding him.

Old-timers' accounts like this unnerved Saalih. On our second visit to Bir Shatuun, he stationed himself atop a steep cliff while I worked below. He was protecting me, he explained; had we been down there together, some Mutayr might have come along and dropped killing-stones on us. I saw some evidence of Mutayr vandalism, or at least an example of how the Khushmaan associate the Mutayr with dishonorable activities. In some caves near Bir Shatuun, Saalih and I discovered a small monastic settlement, dating perhaps from the sixth century. This community's focal point was a church containing once-magnificent frescoes of Christ and angels. The figures had been hideously disfigured by vandals who proudly scrawled their names on what plaster remained. Haamid and his friends were Mutayr, Saalih was sure: no other people would do such a thing.

The Khushmaan judge those cultures that violate fundamental Bedouin taboos as inferior. Cannibalism is the foremost prohibition. I asked my Khushmaan companions whether there were any circumstances in which they would eat human flesh and then related how plane-crash survivors in the high Andes had eaten dead passengers. In no event would they practice cannibalism, they concurred. They despised "Slaves" (ʿAabid), the blacks who worked in the English desert patrols, as man-eaters:

> Long ago the Maʿaza traveled regularly by camel between Safaga and Zaʿafarana. There was once a policeman, a black man, traveling this route with a Khushaymi named Hajj Rafiiʿa Salmaan. They were at the Hawashiyya outflow, where they had millet and lentils for food. But the black man grew hungry. He told Hajj Rafiiʿa, "If you bring me a *ratl* [.45 kg, about 1 lb.] of human meat, I will pay you any price." Thereafter, Hajj Rafiiʿa slept with his rifle, far away from the cannibal.

About a century ago, the nomads relate, a man in Qena ate the breasts and other flesh of his recently deceased wife. In 1962, they say, in the upper Egyptian village of Daraw a "tall woman of dark skin, not respected by her fellow villagers," dug up a recently buried man at night and ate his flesh. The nomads claim that, like the "Slaves," most cannibals hail from the Sudan. A people near Umdurman reportedly eat rather than bury their dead, and neighboring groups must guard their cemeteries against these ghouls. The Takarna, another Sudanese group, venture forth at night to kill and eat humans.

The Maʿaza recognize other taboos that distinguish them from other peoples. Eating any "dogs" (*kilaab*), a category that includes all carnivores, is forbidden. A Khushaymi described the consequences for the *Bani Maklab*, a Sudanese group who tried to tempt the Prophet Muhammad to violate this taboo:

> The males have faces like men, but bodies like dogs. The women are normal. They are Sons of Adam [*Bani Aadam*]. The Prophet once was

their guest. They slaughtered a dog and brought its meat to the Prophet and said "eat it." The Prophet knew it was a dog. He shouted "ish!" [the command "scram!" to a sheep] and nothing happened. He shouted "ikh!" ["scram!" to a goat] and nothing happened. Finally, he shouted "hayya!" ["scram!" to a dog] and the meat jumped off his plate. The Prophet turned all the men into dogs. But he spared the women because one of them had warned him, "Beware the meat the men will bring you."

Even practicing nomads and some people who are nominally Bedouins by virtue of having descended from former nomads have violated the Arabs' taboos. The ʿAwaazim tribe of the Nile Valley near Esna eat foxes, jackals, hyenas, and domestic dogs, according to the Khushmaan. The ʿAbabda eat meat raw and drink unboiled goat's milk. "I once offered an ʿAbadi some raw sheep's liver," Saalih said, "for him to take home and cook. But he ate it on the spot. The ʿAbabda are unsound people."

Proper use of the environment is another standard by which the Bedouins judge humanity. In Wadi Guurdhi we came across a living acacia tree which had been chopped up a year earlier, presumably to feed camels. My companions blamed the Sumayniyya, a clan of the ʿAbabda. They were notorious in the past for making charcoal from live acacias on the limestone plateau adjacent to the Nile Valley. In Wadi Shatuun we found burned acacias whose firing was attributed to the Mutayr Arabs. "Sons of dogs!" Muhammad Umbaarak cursed them.

Where survival is always an issue and hospitality is at a premium, stingy, life-threatening behavior is condemned. The Khushmaan call their southern neighbors "leathern" (*jilda*) in this respect. "If you were dying of thirst here near the ʿAdayd water and a Bishari came to your 'rescue,' he would tell you that the nearest water was at adh-Dhahal" (20 mi., or 32 km, distant), one man said. Although not in danger, Saalih had an experience of this kind with an ʿAbadi woman. He was south of the Edfu-Mersa Alam road when he met this woman and asked her where he could find water. She directed him several kilometers away. "I found out later that as she spoke there was a water source nearly at our feet." Non-Bedouins also have apparently been victims of this ʿAbabda deception. The geographer John Ball, at the turn of the century, wrote that nomads were reluctant to point out water sources, "especially in arid parts of Ababda country" (Ball 1912, 243). Such anecdotes and the historical enmity between the tribes explain why "ʿAbabda" is a common Maʿaza insult. Gently bouncing his year-old daughter on his lap, Umtayr Muhammad teasingly asked her if she were an ʿAbadi. Sulimaan Saalih looked at an unflattering picture I took of him and myself with a flash at night and said, "We look like ʿAbabda!"

3. A Desert Livelihood

On my second trip with the Khushmaan, we were accompanied by a pleasant outdoorsman from Cairo. He came well prepared for his desert journey. Saalih chuckled about the butane cylinders this man brought as cooking fuel. "Nobody realizes," Saalih said, "that people are born and die here, and know how to live and what to eat." Outsiders' curiosity and skepticism about what Bedouins do for a living is well founded: nothing comes easily to the nomads.

Nomadism

Nomads are nomadic because the environments they live in could not support them if they were settled. They live in some of the most marginal, resource-poor habitats in the world, and almost without exception they are the only people who live in such areas. It is generally safe to assume that if nomads were displaced, or had never existed, no one else would live where they do.

Not all nomads (people who migrate regularly) are pastoralists (people who keep domesticated livestock). Migrating in search of wild game and plant food—hunting and gathering—is humanity's oldest occupation. This livelihood is still practiced today by groups such as the Bushmen of Africa's Kalahari Desert. The life-style of pastoral nomadism, in contrast to that of hunting and gathering, is no more than twelve thousand years old. By definition it is dependent upon the herding of animals such as sheep, goats, cattle, and camels, which had not been domesticated before 10,000 B.C. An intriguing question is why people did not tame, breed, and use wild animals earlier than they did.

There is no certain explanation for why people began cultivating wheat and barley and keeping sheep and goats. Apparently, nomadic hunters and gatherers from time immemorial led a prosperous enough existence that they did not need or want the supplemental food that domestic animals and plants represented. Stresses produced by population growth or climatic changes may have forced some of these groups in the Middle East to find new ways of coping.

Pastoral nomadism is widely regarded as an incidental offshoot of early agricultural life. Few authorities disagree fundamentally with the geographer Carl Sauer, who proposed that "as the numbers of people and livestock increased, herdsmen and herd moved farther and farther away from the villages and became more permanently detached from the settled lands. This about describes the roots of pastoral nomadism" (1952, 97). Archeology for the most part supports the idea that captive breeding of sheep and goats occurred only after people domesticated cereals and settled down to farm in the mountains of southwest Asia; however, in some sites sheep remains predate those of cultivated cereal. Some authorities believe that the wild progenitors of sheep and goats could not resist feeding in fields and stores of cultivated wheat and barley (Reed 1977, 561). The animals' contact with sedentary farmers—the only people who had surplus food capable of sustaining captive animals—eventually led to the domestication of these animals (Ucko and Dimbleby 1954, 273).

Many groups of hunter-gatherers and pastoral nomads around the world pride themselves on their independence, their intimacy with nature, and their relatively prosperous standard of living, measured by what they consider to be quality of life. There is no evidence of hunter-gatherers ever having starved to death (Heathcote 1983, 139). Anthropologist Richard Lee found that the hunting and gathering Bushmen of the Kalahari, without having to walk very far or work very hard, enjoy a subsistence that is "at least routine and reliable and at best surprisingly abundant" (Lee 1968, 30, 39).

Pastoral nomads have also historically been well-off in this unconventional sense, despite terrible setbacks like the Sahel drought of the 1970s. Of the nomads of Iran, Afghanistan, and Pakistan, the anthropologist Fredrik Barth reported that "a comparison of nomadic and settled communities in their present forms reveals a clear difference in the average standard of living in favour of the nomad camp" (Barth 1962, 353).[1] Barth noted that for this reason the nomads were reluctant to settle and were likely to do so only if they become destitute, for example, because of drought.

Some nomads do settle, either by choice or force. Those who choose to settle typically do so because of economic or ecological factors working against them. Many who settle do not turn their backs entirely on their formerly nomadic ways, but develop new ways of exploiting both the desert and the sown. Pastoral nomads, or more accurately people who refer to themselves as nomads, choose from a wide array of possible economic activities, on a continuum ranging from a desert way of life in which they have only brief trade contacts with agricultural communities, to an almost completely agricultural existence in which they have only nominal affinities with desert people, but continue to call themselves "Arabs" or Bedouins (Johnson 1969, 12).[2]

Khushmaan families span this continuum, with about half the clan, or 125 families (approximately 900 people), practicing the desert-based way of life described in this text; about seven households (or perhaps 50 people) occupying a midway point of using desert resources and visiting desert kin on a regular basis and exploiting desert resources while maintaining fixed residences in villages and towns; and approximately 125 families leading wholly agricultural lives. The desert people with few exceptions consider temporary wage labor in towns or for townspeople as a normal, acceptable pursuit, especially in times of drought.

For at least seventy-five years, most desert-dwelling Khushmaan men have worked briefly as guards for oil installations, railways, and other utilities and as road builders and miners, earning up to $260 (210 £E) per month, while their wives and children remained in the desert with the family's livestock. Some men like Saalih Sulimaan, guard for an oil pump station on the coastal plain near Ras Gharib, are fortunate enough to have their families and herds in the desert close to their place of work. The fully settled Khushmaan keep water buffalo and sheep and grow crops in the Nile Valley, living on the desert edge in villages such as Hamaadha (ash-Shimayda) near al-Minya. Their seminomadic peers maintain residences in these same villages, but while the women tend crops and keep small animals, the men pasture camels on the desert edge and travel regularly into the desert to mine salt and harvest wormwood, ben-seeds, and other wild products. They are regarded by their more sedentary and more nomadic peers alike as the wealthiest of all the Khushmaan.

This apparently smooth continuum belies the antagonism between settled and nomadic life perceived by the nomads themselves. The desert-dwelling Khushmaan believe that their kin who have settled have compromised themselves by taking on peasant ways, even if they do maintain nominal contacts with the desert. Saalih lamented to me that the eleven-year-old son of a desert man who had settled in a Red Sea coastal town about the time his son was born did not even know the Khushmaan clan "signature" (*wasm*). Kinspeople who have settled are regarded as avaricious and greedy, qualities which the nomads decry. Regardless of income, the desert people do not want steady work because they regard it as subservience to others. The desert nomads' perceptions that agriculturalists are their opposites and that settled life is inferior prevent many of these desert people from changing their traditional ways, even when environmental and economic incentives to settle are strong. In view of this folk perception of the dichotomy between the desert and the sown and its important influence on behavior, it seems inappropriate to endorse a recent academic consensus that this dichotomy has been exaggerated or no longer exists.[3]

A common misperception among sedentary people is that there are "true" nomads who lead their lives entirely in the wilderness, avoiding all contact with "civilization." In reality no pastoral nomads have ever been entirely independent of settled communities. The pastoral nomadic livelihood depends upon a symbiotic relationship between the nomads and farming people: the nomads supply livestock and other desert produce to villages and towns, and markets in these settlements provide the nomads with goods that cannot be produced in the desert, such as tea, sugar, flour, rice, lentils, and cloth. In addition, these market towns are indispensable as centers for exchange of information about environmental conditions in the desert interior. The head of a desert family must travel to town once every six or eight weeks to obtain supplies. His principal contact in town is the clan *shaykh* who resides there permanently. The visitor tells his headman about the status of water, pasture, and game in the region he just came from and in other areas he passed through. Every visitor supplies the *shaykh* with this kind of information, so that he is always able to advise his clansmen where the best and worst conditions are to be found. On this basis the nomads often make their decisions about when and where to relocate. Other places such as the oil-pumping station where a Bedouin works for a few months or even years likewise serve as centers of information exchange.

Sedentary people have seldom recognized the advantages of nomadic existence and by coercion and enticement have tried to settle nomads. Raising the nomads' standard of living is a common justification. Settled people tend to view simple material possessions and rag-tag clothing as signs of poverty and environmental skills such as hunting and tracking as indications of a "primitive" culture. Some authorities feel that "the nomads must catch up with the caravan of modern civilization" by becoming farmers and industrial workers.[4] Less altruistic motives, particularly on the part of governments, are behind other efforts to settle nomads.[5]

Assailed by the fears, biases, and policies of settled people, nomadism is on the retreat. Estimates of the total number of the world's pastoral nomads in 1980 ranged from 5 to 13 million persons, or 0.8 to 2.1 percent of the total population of the world's arid lands. This represents a decline from an estimated 20 million nomads in 1960 (Heathcote 1983, 143, 134). That nomads, both hunter-gatherers and pastoralists, have largely succumbed by choice or force to sedentary ways does not mean their livelihoods have proven unviable in the twentieth century. They have persisted successfully from prehistoric times and would be more widespread today if not for the interventions of urban and industrial societies.

Pastoral Activities

The Khushmaan who dwell in the desert raise sheep, goats, and camels. They also hunt, collect edible and marketable wild plants, cultivate crops, and work for wages. Like many other pastoral nomads whom observers long regarded exclusively as pastoralists, the Khushmaan thus practice "multi-resource nomadism."[6] While activities such as hunting and gathering are especially important in times of drought, when food and water for livestock are in short supply, pastoralism is nevertheless the nomads' chief preoccupation.

Sheep and Goats

Income from the sale of sheep and goats is the backbone of the Khushmaan economy. The nomads herd their surplus male and older female animals to the Qena-Safaga road or Ras Gharib–Hurghada road, then flag down a vehicle and escort the animals to Qena's Thursday market or Qoseir's Friday market. Alternatively, they sell livestock to one of the Khushmaan car owners who resells them at a 50 percent markup. Villagers and townspeople buy and butcher the animals. From an average herd of fifty animals, the family in a year of fair pasture sells off the surplus of some twenty goats at $31 (25 £E) each and ten sheep at $69 (55 £E) each; the family's average annual pastoral income is about $800 (650 £E).

Sheep and goats do well in the desert, although they are not as fully adapted to hot, dry conditions as is the camel. A sheep maintains an almost constant body temperature and, unlike the camel, must pant rather than sweat. Its thick fleece, however, offers fine insulation from desert heat, and both sheep and goats can survive a 30 percent weight loss through dehydration (Cloudsley-Thompson 1977, 110, 152). The normal life span of sheep and goats is ten to twelve years.

As a grazing animal, the sheep has a much better reputation among non-pastoralists than the browsing and grazing goat. For its ravenous appetite and capacity to remove vegetation, outsiders have labeled the goat a devilish "hooved locust" and "ecological dominant" (Thirgood 1981, 68). The Bedouins, on the other hand, regard the goat as an extraordinary animal that makes it possible for people to live in the desert. Admitting that goats do destroy small plants, the Khushmaan point out that they do not harm adult vegetation and, unlike ibex, do not dig plants out by the roots. Furthermore, the Bedouins point out, in a spring following good rains, the average goat herd generates about twenty-five pounds (11 kg) of milk for human consumption each day, something sheep cannot do.

Having a mixed herd of sheep and goats is a deliberate Khushmaan strategy for reducing risks and maximizing benefits.[7] The nomads point out that if one kept only goats, many or all of the animals might die if exposed to the mysterious disease described below. With only sheep, there would be no milk or cheese for people. Hyenas, which occasionally foray in wintertime over the Khushmaan desert, prey almost exclusively on sheep, and a family owning only sheep could lose everything to the marauder.

Ironically, the Ma'aza cannot pasture their goats on mountain slopes, the habitat best suited to these hooved climbers. "They die there for some reason," Saalih said:

> The goats get sick with *adh-dhibaar* fourteen days after they've been in the mountains. There is swelling in the shoulders, back, and chest; the animal is listless and eats little or nothing and soon dies. If you took a hundred head into the mountains of Ghaarib, Gattaar, or Galaala for a month, they would all die this way. You could let them drink once and leave, and there would be no problem. You cannot take goats to the Ghaarib water to drink because they will die, but you can carry the water to them below to drink and nothing will happen. So it's not the water at fault but something else. A lot of people say it is from the ibex, but this is not true. The goats get sick only in ibex country, but there are some places like Jidhaami, Muwayh, 'Atulla, and Umm Haadh where ibex live that goats don't get sick. Some say there are seasons when goats become ill. My uncle Sulimaan Suwaylim thought it was the stinging of a blue wasp in daylight that poisoned goats; you could water your goats at night and they wouldn't get sick, nor would your sheep, maybe because the wasp couldn't sting through their coats.

Noting these symptoms, medical zoologist Dr. Harry Hoogstraal suggested that the culprit might be a malaria-like disease caused by a tick-borne protozoan.[8] Ibex are apparently immune to this malady. Another possibility, said Hoogstraal, is that this is a kind of sleeping sickness, caused by trypanosomes carried by the small hippoboscid flies that plague both ibex and goats in the Eastern Desert. Whatever the cause, this disease is a frustrating reality for the Arabs, whose range would be wider and economy stronger were their goats able to inhabit the mountains.

There is a strict sexual division of labor in Khushmaan animal herding. While tending camels is men's work, herding sheep and goats is the duty of women and children. At dawn they drive the herd out of camp toward pasture and usually do not return until nightfall. Nominally, sheep and goats belong not to individuals but to the Khushmaan clan and bear the Khushmaan signature (*wasm*) of a sliced ear. In fact, livestock are the property of particular families and individuals. As her security in case of divorce, the household mother owns some animals, and others are designated as children's property.

Sheep and goats have enormous cultural as well as practical value for the Goat People. Goat's milk is emblematic of the best things in life, the health and independence people enjoy when the desert is in bloom. There is no greater way to honor a guest than to slaughter a sheep or kid for him. The animal is killed and dressed in churchlike silence and eaten in a spirit of communion. Except for the spontaneous celebration of an honored visitor, these feasts are prepared only for such important occasions as weddings, circumcisions, or funeral observances. Although the Bedouins are stock-raisers, meat is an infrequent item in their diet, for regular consumption would quickly bring economic ruin.

Camels and Donkeys

The Khushmaan now keep camels for draft rather than breeding purposes, and so the days of large family herds of up to fifty animals are gone. Most families own one to four camels. A few households have ten to fifteen, and one man owns twenty-five camels. The nomads sell their few surplus animals in the Sunday Market of Qena or in Daraw. Some of these find their way to the camel *suq* in the Cairo suburb of Imbaba, where they are bought to be butchered for meat. Between 1950 and 1955 the finest camel could be purchased for $25 (20 £E). By 1962 the going price was $44 (35 £E), and in 1984 was $625 (500 £E).

Its low numbers and apparently minimal economic importance belies the camel's value to the Khushmaan. Although the Bedouins have few possessions, there are always people, baggage, and water that need hauling. The camel is unsurpassed in performing these tasks and works from four years of age, or about halfway to maturity, until the advanced age of twenty-five. Males are better for riding, but both sexes can carry loads of up to 330 pounds (150 kg). At a pace of about two and a half miles an hour (4 KPH) the camel can march twenty-five miles (40 km) in a day, the Arabs claim. Weigall reported that riding camels bore his police officers at four-and-a-half miles per hour (7.25 KPH), easily covering up to thirty miles (48 km) (Weigall 1909, 25). The camel's all-out speed is ten miles per hour (16 KPH) (Cloudsley-Thompson 1977, 104).

Due to their high cost and limited numbers, camels are seldom slaughtered; occasionally, a wealthy herdsman will sacrifice an animal at a wedding or other large gathering. After camel meat, camel milk is the most esteemed item in the nomads' diet. "Camels' milk is the Arabs' intoxicant," Sulimaan Mara'i recited an old Bedouin rhyme. Muhammad Umbaarak added that after drinking camel's milk for fifteen days, without any other food or beverage, a person remains fit and strong. Sulimaan Maraʿi responded with an account of the good old days, beginning with "I drank plenty of camel's milk in my day!"

Camels are the most important property bearing the clan signature. If the animal is born in a Khushmaan herd, this brand, resembling the letter H, is applied when the camel is a year old. The Khushmaan believe the best camels are those bred by the Bisharin tribesmen, so they sometimes travel to the camel market in Daraw to obtain these. In many cases the animals are already branded with other tribal signatures and will not be marked with the Khushmaan *wasm*.

The Khushmaan are close to their camels and give them personal names, such as ʿIfaashaa ("Gatherer") and Dharaʿa ("Traveler") for females, Balhaan ("Sphinx") and Sinaan ("Spearhead") for males. They have a remarkable inventory of terms for camels' sex, age, color, and numbers, and even for the size, color, consistency, and age of camel dung. Regarding them as clean ruminating animals, the Bedouins often stroke and kiss their camels' muzzles and eat bread cooked in camel-dung "briquettes." Inevitably, camels are prominent in the Arabs' folklore and imagination. Adults enjoy telling children that the animal's breast-pad (*zurr al-jamal*) is a spare leg which will grow out if any appendage falls off or is broken. They say that God has one hundred names, the hundredth known only by the camel (Tregenza 1955, 234).

The Arabs are experts on camel behavior. We once came across a line of six cairns, each about five feet (1.5 m) high, located at about fifteen-foot (5 m) intervals across a canyon floor. My companions explained the purpose of these mysterious stone piles: they were "ghosts" (*zawwaal*), in effect scarecrows to frighten any wayward camel into turning back toward camp. The Bedouins explained that the camel is not afraid of what moves, but is frightened by any object it has not seen before in a particular place and which does not move, including a man if he stands still for several minutes. With "ghosts," the owner can give his animal limited freedom to roam and feed, a method intermediate between hobbling the camel and leaving it to its own devices.

Camels are usually good-natured, but have a sometimes-deserved reputation for being mean. One of the worst incidents was the death of the ʿAbadi ʿAmm Naasir Haamid in Wadi Umsikat al-Juukh in the 1970s. Male camels become particularly aggressive during the spring mating season, and that was when ʿAmm Naasir whipped his bull-camel for some offense. The vengeful animal turned on him, biting his head, shoulders, and neck; ʿAmm Naasir died less than thirty minutes later. One of Saalih's camels once bit his hand severely, thinking Saalih was about to strike him. An angry camel sometimes throws a rider with the intention of harming him. ʿAwaad Saliim lost a young son this way.

The camel is extraordinarily well adapted to the desert, especially in its economical use of water. It does not need to drink any water during winters when green pasture is abundant; George Murray recorded one of his camels going 128 days without water (1967, 27). In the most extreme summer conditions, it must drink once every five days, while sheep and donkeys must have water every second day and goats every third. A camel can drink over 30 percent of its body weight in one draft, up to thirty-two gallons (120 liters) for an 880-pound (400 kg) female and forty gallons (150 liters) for an 1,100-pound (500 kg) male (Schmidt-Nielsen 1964, 67). In turn, the camel can sustain a 30 percent loss of body weight through dehydration without ill effect; in comparison, a loss of 12 percent is fatal to man (Cloudsley-Thompson 1977, 103). Reducing the loss of water, rather than storing it, is the key to the camel's success. The body temperature is not fixed as in most mammals but fluctuates. In daytime it rises, allowing heat to be stored and reducing the camel's need to sweat; at night the body temperature decreases and heat is lost.

One problem in keeping such a large domesticated animal is gaining its trust that you will supply it with food, so that it will stay with you. If there is plenty of pasture near camp, this is not a problem; like goats, camels feed on almost everything growing. In barren areas, however, an unhobbled camel will move off to feed. In their management of the animal, the Khushmaan take advantage of another of the camel's extraordinary traits: its way-finding ability. The nomads claim that the animal never forgets a route traveled or water source visited. Once it learns the country, a camel is never reluctant to wander on its own. During times of drought, when herding the animals to sufficient pasture and water becomes difficult, the Khushmaan turn camels loose to fend for themselves; these camels are called *haamil* (pl. *hamal*), or "left to their own devices." The animals manage well, covering great expanses of the Eastern Desert searching for food and drinking water at the two "open" sources of Araas and Gattaar Abu Tarfa. After a few weeks, months, or even a year or two, when the owner wants his camel back he begins tracking it. There are few enough Khushmaan camels so that almost any Khushaymi can recognize a particular Khushmaan animal by its appearance and tracks. People tell the tracker, "I saw your camel's tracks over in Wadi such-and-such this many days ago"; there the owner can pick up the trail and finally locate the animal. Camels that have been left to their own devices for extended periods are skittish but are soon lured back into human company. They have never become feral in the Ma'aza desert, as they have in the Australian outback.

The most common Khushmaan explanation for why they do not have more camels is that it is physically taxing for people to manage them. In summer the owner may have to haul water frequently from remote sources to his camels. Daily chores like hobbling and pasturing the animals are daunting. I asked why people did not build up herds of fifty camels and ease the burden by leaving them *haamil*. The answer: unattended camels have since 1968 been targets of malicious or hungry soldiers stationed in desert outposts or on maneuvers; many others have died in unfenced minefields, including seven at Bir al-Basha alone.

Unfortunately for the Khushmaan, the camel is better adapted to sandy than stony deserts. This animal has great difficulties negotiating steep inclines and loose rocks and is generally left below when people go into the mountains. Fortunately there is an alternative animal in these circumstances.

In mountainous areas and for poor families, the donkey substitutes for the tasks usually performed by the stronger, more drought-tolerant and more expensive camel. The donkey's body temperature does not fluctuate as much as the camel's, and its summer water expenditure may be three to four times that of the camel. However, the donkey is superior on steep and rocky terrain and costs only about $60–$120 (50–100 £E). For these reasons, most families own at least one donkey.

Perhaps because they are the objects of food prohibition in Islam and vulgar jokes in folk culture, donkeys are often abused in Egypt. Even Khushmaan donkeys have been victimized. In 1970 army soldiers killed four in Wadi Safaga for no apparent reason. Due to this danger and the donkey's inclination to become feral, as a large wild herd on the South Galala Plateau attests, the Arabs seldom leave the animals untended.

Drought and Nonpastoral Activities

Measures of Drought

The Bedouin home is a landscape of uncertainty and anticipation. The nomads' economy, and indeed entire way of life, is based on the assumption that wild fodder for livestock is or will soon be obtainable somewhere. However, prolonged drought periodically reigns, and the nomads' good life vanishes. "The country has died" is what the Khushmaan say about an area seared by drought. During these periods, the Bedouins wait and take comfort from images of the past and hoped-for new beginnings: spring seasons when wadis are buried in verdure, livestock are satiated, waterskins are filled with milk, and rock basins are brimful of water. One nomad's comment on a barren gravel plain called "Rivulets of the Young Camels" (Raydhaan al-Abkaar) conveys this sense of contrast between surplus and want: "This place once saw abundant vegetation, and milk, and camels. People would go to Qena from here to fetch grain when they needed it. They watered the animals at Umm Diisa, every six or seven days, so plentiful was the pasture. This was in the days of Sulimaan Suwaylim and Sulimaan ʿAwda, who brought their camels to this place. At one time three hundred to five hundred camels were here to enjoy the pasture. Now, there is nothing."

The Khushmaan point to several indications of severe, in contrast to normal, drought. Persistent, widespread aridity harms even those animals that normally cope by tolerating rather than by avoiding drought. The Bedouins' nickname for the gazelle is "heedless one" (*jaazy*) because it never drinks water directly. Unable to find seasonal pasture or the acacia's perennial nourishment, gazelles may die, say the nomads, from eating nonsucculent, salty plants such as *gilu* (*Anabasis setifera*). Other animals suffer. The ibex must drink; it perishes when surface water is unavailable throughout its range. During one desiccated spring season, Muhammad Umbaarak captured with his bare hands a young adult male which, he said, was weakened by drought.

The nomads' greatest concern is for their livestock. Khushmaan shepherds say that sheep and goats deprived of *hurbith* (*Lotononis platycarpa*) and other nutritious green plants and forced to subsist on dried forage such as *diriis* (desiccated *Zilla spinosa*) lose weight and fall ill. During drought, a young camel "can resemble a very old camel," and any camel deprived of green fodder becomes "short-tempered." Saalih observed the anger of one of his camels: "He is mad now because he cannot eat green plants." There is barely or not enough milk to sustain newborn animals and none for human consumption. Many animals die; for example, during the 1956–59 drought, Umtayr Silmi lost about thirty head of sheep, more than half his herd.

When pasture is scarce, supplementary food is expensive. Each camel requires up to four-and-a-half pounds (2 kg) of flour cakes and grain daily to complement a meager diet of dried *Zilla spinosa* and other desert forage. A ewe may eat up to $13 (10 £E) of flour monthly; with an average of ten ewes in a herd the expense is $125 (100 £E) per month, an investment that may go for nought if they die.

Long droughts confront the nomads with difficult choices. One option is to abandon the nomadic way of life and take up farming in the Nile Valley or to settle in Red Sea towns as laborers. Saalih spoke about the effects of a great drought in the Eastern Desert between 1943 and 1958:

> In 1956 we wanted to die from hunger. I was with my brother Salmaan. We had no money to buy food. Everyone was affected. People took to cutting wormwood to sell. Then the wormwood was almost gone.
> I worked laying asphalt on the Hurghada-Safaga road, nine hours a day, from five o'clock in the morning, for twenty cents [16 P.T.]. Oh, Protector, it was something foul! There was no cash to buy grain to feed the animals. The wasted sheep and goats were worth only a quarter

of their value in good health. Hajj Umtayr and others settled in the Nile Valley and stayed there because the drought made them so angry they wouldn't return.

Permanent settlement is not the only choice nomads have. Some Middle Eastern pastoralists have been known to relocate in settled communities for several years before returning to the desert; they are "nomads on the waiting list" (Salzman 1980, 13).[9] Khushmaan families that left the desert have never returned to desert life in this fashion. The desert-dwelling Khushmaan believe that settling down is an irreversible move and have developed a number of ways to avoid abandoning their desert ways permanently, especially when drought threatens them. During the drought of 1975–1985, for example, the Bedouins sustained themselves through a combination of nonpastoral and nonnomadic activities which, in better times, are only incidental features in their economy. These include collecting wild plants, hunting, growing crops, and working for wages.

Plant Collecting

Annual or ephemeral plants cannot survive prolonged drought. While these drought-avoiding plants fail, however, drought-enduring perennials thrive. When rain does not fall the Bedouins turn to perennial shrubs and woody trees like the acacia for sustenance. One nomad called the acacia "life" itself: "In times of drought, *sayaal* is the best plant. . . . It lives whether there is rain or not. . . . It is good for the camel, hyrax, ibex, gazelle, sheep, and goat, which eat its seed pods, flowers, and leaves. . . . It gives man edible gum, poles for the wool house, wood for camel saddles, bark for curing waterskins, and shade."

The nomads imitate nature to sustain their domestic animals during dry spells. Gazelles and ibex in times of drought feed on acacia leaves blown to the ground and on perennial shrubs. During prolonged drought, families congregate around places where such perennial trees and shrubs are especially abundant. There, people replicate the natural action of wind by using a camel staff (*mahjan*) to shake loose acacia and other leaves to feed their sheep and goats.[10] Perennial shrubs sustain the Khushmaan in other ways. The foliage and seeds of some species are highly sought-after in the folk pharmacies and spice bazaars of the Nile Valley. One of these, wormwood (*baʿaytharaan, Artemesia judaica*), is closely related to the fragrant sage of western America's chaparral country. Egyptians burn this *shiih* to enjoy its aroma and spread it about the house to drive off snakes, scorpions, and other vermin. "*Shiih* in the house is a good thing" goes an old adage.

Wormwood is the most readily collected of the wild plants, for it is widespread in both the limestone and granitic regions of the Eastern Des-

ert. It does not grow densely, but by covering much ground a man is able
to harvest enough wormwood to contribute significantly to his family's income. He cuts selected stems, leaving roots and some foliage to ensure re-
generation, and places the cuttings in the sun. Five to ten days later he
separates leaves from stems and packs the dried foliage into burlap sacks
for transport by a middleman's camel or car to market. Sold to the middleman at thirty cents per pound (50 P.T./kg), wormwood is available in
Cairo for $1.40 per pound (2.50 £E/kg).

Ben-trees (*yasar, Moringa peregrina*) grow only on the lower flanks of
mountains higher than 4,900 feet (1,500 m), for only such high peaks catch
enough moisture to meet the trees' needs. Their starkly white bark and
long wispy needles characterize the Eastern Desert's unique montane atmosphere. In late autumn Khushmaan men converge on the uplands to
harvest ben-seeds from the long pods that hang from *yasar* branches. It is a
time for socializing and hard work. Two to five men work together, pull-
ing at what pods they can reach and throwing rocks to dislodge others. At
day's end they gather their separate piles together and begin separating
seeds from husks. They fill as many burlap sacks as possible, each containing about 120 pounds (55 kg) of seeds. Desert middlemen purchase the
seeds for fifty-five cents per pound (1 £E/kg), and Cairo shoppers pay
$3.40 a pound (6 £E/kg). Ben-seeds have been valued in the Nile Valley
and beyond since Ptolemaic times for their fine oil. Today, women buy this
baan, fustug baan, or *habb ghaaliya* with the reported purpose of eating
the seeds to become fatter and therefore more beautiful. Ben-oil is also
prized by watchmakers (Watt and Breyer-Brandwijk 1962, 781).

Argel (*harjal, Solenostemma arghel*) leaves are boiled for tea by both
townspeople and Bedouins to settle the stomach. This hardy shrub is far
scarcer than wormwood and fetches a higher price; the Bedouins sell it to
middlemen at $1.70 per pound (3 £E/kg), and it costs twice that for the
Cairo consumer. Uncropped argel plants are difficult to find, and nomads
admit that they sometimes do not give the plants adequate time to regen-
erate leaves before harvesting them.

There is a very limited demand in the Nile Valley for the leaves of Egyptian henbane (*Hyoscyamus boveanus*), the source of pharmaceutical hyoscya-
mine and a cheap intoxicant in Nile villages. This *saykaraan*, named after
the Arabic root meaning "to become drunk," was despised by the Bedouins
who once harvested it in quantity: "After half a day cutting the stuff your
head was turned upside down," one complained.

It is difficult to establish how much income the plant harvest brings
to the Khushmaan. The nomads estimated their combined harvest of
wormwood in 1983 at one hundred tons, for a net worth of $2,810 (2,250
£E); of ben-seeds that year at two tons, worth $2,275 (1,820 £E). In seven-
teen days Saalih and 'Awaad Umtayr harvested 330 pounds (150 kg) of ben-

seeds for a total revenue of $188 (150 £E); each man earned an average of $5.50 (4.40 £E) per day. Saalih estimated that by working hard for ten days a man could harvest 175 pounds (80 kg) of wormwood, thus making an average $5 (4 £E) per day. As wage-earners guarding oil equipment or building roads, the Bedouins by comparison earn an average $3.75 (3 £E) per day. Wage labor is possible year-round, while the wild harvest is subject to seasonal and other environmental limitations. The nomads, however, prefer desert work not only for greater income but for the freedom it offers, so few miss any opportunity to collect plants.

Hunting

Two features of their material culture distinguish the Khushmaan from most other pastoral nomads of the late twentieth century: the almost-complete absence of automobiles and the total lack of firearms. Without these amenities the Bedouins have developed exceptional hunting skills, or rather have never lost them.

The Ma'aza were not always without guns. Early in the 1800s, John Wilkinson noted they were better armed than their rival 'Ababda tribesmen (Wilkinson 1832, 32). Before 1910, according to Russell, a few Ma'aza and "other predatory Arabs of the desert edge" owned antiquated Remington and Martini rifles (1949, 34). 'Awaad Saliim in the 1940s told Tregenza that in his earlier days, when no firearms permit was required, he had shot many ibex (1955, 150). The nomads relate that after about 1930 guns were prohibited completely. The ban has occasionally been reinforced, most recently following the assassination of the Egyptian leader Anwar al-Sadat.

Today the Khushmaan have no guns. The government, concerned about the potential threat posed by such a mobile force, will not grant them firearms permits. They lack even bows and arrows or spears. Their hunting technology is rudimentary and employs techniques identical to those used in the area seven thousand years ago during the Neolithic Age.

One "Neolithic" device is the sand partridge trap (*mirdaaha*). Four stones are buried in sand with their tops at ground level to form a square enclosure about six inches deep and twelve inches across. A few lentils or other grains are scattered on the floor of this enclosure. Two sticks are then laid horizontally to form a V, and at their apex one is propped atop the other. Upon this apex a stick is placed vertically to support a heavy flat stone that is wider than the enclosure. A sand partridge enters the dugout to feed and soon bumps against one of the V-sticks, bringing down the roof. Recovered alive, the bird is slaughtered ritually and eaten.

'Atulla Mara'i devised his own ingenious method for hunting sand-grouse. He surrounded the lip of a water basin at Jebel Abu Harba with limbs of ben-trees, which have a smooth bark. In order to reach the water, the thirsty birds were obliged to stand on the wood, and many slipped in. ʿAtulla checked the water regularly to retrieve the struggling birds.

Throughout the Eastern Desert, there are Neolithic rock drawings of ibex hunts. I saw the nomads reenact these very scenes on numerous occasions in the 1980s. Once Saalih and I were trailing two Tababna companions, Hilayil and Afrayj, and their dog Hawaash up ʿAdayd Canyon in the South Galala Plateau. There was commotion ahead of us, and we ran to catch up. Hawaash had scared up a young male ibex as it was feeding on the canyon floor. Characteristically the wild goat bounded toward the cliffs and began climbing.

The men would have lost their quarry at this point if not for their dog. The canine makes the hunt Neolithic rather than Paleolithic, for dogs were domesticated only within the past twenty thousand years. Had the cliff been steeper the ibex would have left its pursuer behind, only pausing periodically to look back. Here Hawaash was able to make some headway up the canyon wall and thus give the hunters an opportunity. Although the ibex could have fled higher to safety, Hilayil explained, it feared that any forward motion would only encourage its pursuer and was confident that by standing its ground it could successfully challenge or at least discourage the predator. Positioned on the same contour and just feet away from one another, the dog barked for its master while the ibex snorted threateningly. In the absence of a huntsman, such a standoff often ends in deadlock, with each animal going its way. Sometimes the impasse ends with the dog seizing its quarry's leg for a while before letting go; and sometimes with the dog's death, as the clever goat charges the dog and with a sweep of its horns spins it from its perch. Muhammad Umtayr explained that even the huntsman is in danger:

> You must be careful handling ibex! The male is especially dangerous. He will first try to pick you up by getting the tips of his horns under your legs or hitting you to knock you off balance. If he gets you down he will crash his forehorns against you until you die. This happened once to a man named Salaama. The ibex crushed his head and chest with its horns. He lived for a few hours and his wounds were treated but he soon died. Any male with horns longer than two hand spans is dangerous like this. If you trap an ibex on a ledge, it will never try to run past you by taking the outside of the ledge. No matter how tightly you hug the wall the ibex will try to wedge himself between you and the wall and try to throw you to your death. That's why it is important to get above the game.

This day, however, as in perhaps a third of all such challenges, the hunting team was successful. Afrayj scrambled above the animals and located a heavy flat stone. The ibex knew he was there but was more concerned

with the dog. Afrayj thus had ample time to position himself carefully before aiming and dropping the rock. Struck hard, the animal tumbled down
into Hilayil's hands. The Arabs quickly killed the ibex in ritual fashion,
cutting its throat and praying, "In the name of God, the Compassionate,
the Merciful." Had the animal died before being slaughtered in this way,
the Bedouins would not have eaten it, as they observe the Islamic law of
ritual sacrifice.

The other principal method of hunting ibex, by wheel trap, has also
been in use since Neolithic times. The trap consists of a palm fiber ring
about six inches (15 cm) across, and stitched into its inner rim is a circle of
inward-pointing palm leaf-ends, or spines of *Acacia raddiana* or *Rhamnus
dispermus*. The pointed leaf or spine tips converge at the circle's center. In
the ground on an animal trail, or near a food or water source, the trapper
excavates a pit about four inches across and twelve deep (10 × 30 cm) and
centers the wheel trap over it. On top of this he places a noose of a simple
slipknot. He attaches the other end of this line to either a notched rock or
a stick, then buries the trap in shallow sand. The ibex or gazelle victim
steps through the noose and palm wheel into the pit below. As the animal
struggles to free itself of the palm spikes irritating its leg, it inadvertently
tightens the slipknot just above the ring. If the end of the rope is attached
to a rock, the animal's only hope is to fight the rope until friction breaks it.
The Khushmaan, recognizing this weakness in the method, prefer tying
off to a free stick rather than an anchor stone. They use an acacia or other
tree limb blackened at each end in a fire. As the animal runs the stick strikes
rocks, leaving an easy trail for the tracker to follow. The stick eventually
becomes lodged among boulders, and the hunter catches up to his prey.

The Khushmaan have learned some of their hunting techniques by
studying Neolithic remains. On our way to the Muwayh water, Saalih and
I followed a well-worn ibex path. At intervals we found the remains of low
rock walls set perpendicularly across the path. Each wall had only one gate
and through it the ibex passed each day. The animals had probably followed this route for thousands of years. Ancient people had discovered
this ibex pathway and had erected the walls we saw. In the gaps they had
set their wheel traps. Saalih was certain that the ancients' snares had been
tied off to anchor stones and began looking for one. He found several buried under the walls near the trap gates. A few hours later at the Muwayh
water, Saalih fashioned a palm ring and, copying the ancient pattern,
notched a rock's midsection to tie off on. He was using a device unaltered
by time, and the anticipation as we watched our prey must have been felt
by others long ago at this very place.

One October day in 1983, I witnessed a Paleolithic hunting scene: even
dogs were absent. Saalih, his son Sulimaan, Muhammad Umbaarak, and I
were camped near the mouth of the Abu Nakhayla Gorge, a great cut run-

ning north out of the South Galala Plateau into the Wadi ʿAraba plain. Early in the morning, we left Muhammad and hiked up a gravel terrace above the main Abu Nakhayla drainage, pausing occasionally to peer down onto the wadi floor. Sulimaan spotted two gazelles feeding below us. His father caught up, surveyed the situation, and whispered to Sulimaan to take up a weapon. Saalih armed himself with an oblong fist-sized rock and edged closer to the canyon wall. He was downwind from the animals, and the upper branches of an acacia partially blocked the view: the gazelles were unaware of him. He crept closer to the canyon wall, then stood and hurled the rock with what he later said was half his might, for more velocity would have diminished his accuracy. I snapped photographs and expected a brief chance to catch the animals fleeing in fear down the canyon. Instead I heard a gazelle's desperate bark and Saalih's shouts for my pocketknife. From thirty-five feet he had pitched his weapon with mortal accuracy, striking the animal's spinal cord.

It was a day of incongruities. Muhammed Umbarak had been in camp listening to the radio. When we finished our excited accounts of the hunt, he told us that a bomb had destroyed the U.S. Marine barracks in Beirut, killing more than two hundred men.

Bedouin hunts of the future might continue to employ techniques proven in ancient times. I heard of a strategy, tried only once, which combined the old and the new. One of the four Khushmaan automobile owners loaded the back of his pickup with about two hundred potato-sized stones and took on three passenger-hunters. Their goal was to overtake or exhaust a gazelle, an animal capable of running fifty miles per hour (80 KPH), and bring it down by throwing stones. They did not find any would-be prey.

Perhaps because of their constant physical activity, the Bedouins crave meat. They await anxiously the next ceremonial slaughter of a sheep or goat. The sudden chance catch of an ibex or gazelle and the thrill of the hunt induce a sense of euphoria unequaled in any aspect of men's social life. While going about the first order of business, skinning the animal and roasting its edible entrails, the hunters excitedly recall all details of the chase: difficulties of the terrain, speed and cleverness of the dog, hysterical orders shouted between men, angry struggle of the quarry. After the liver is salted and given to the honored guest, or divided up among partners, serious eating begins. A large portion of meat is boiled and divided. Dessert is *fatta*, a rich mixture of meat broth, ghee, and freshly baked bread. Sleep follows.

Gazelle meat has a consistent quality reminiscent of the tenderest dark turkey portions. Ibex has a more variable texture, ranging from that of tender mutton to stringy beef and pure fat. The Bedouins have a unanimous preference, conveyed by a man who observed: "The morning after you eat ibex, your mouth, joints, and muscles are sore, tired. It's hard for you to get up. But two, three, or seven days later, you are strong and can almost run up mountains without tiring. Ibex meat is something strange, unusual. Gazelle meat is like regular food, ghee or cheese or dates, but the ibex, oh! It is something else!"

The nomads waste none of the animal. Heart, lungs, stomach, intestines, testicles, brain, and even the muscles of the face are eaten. Fat is often retained as a snack called *ash-shaham:* boiled with salt, suet is packed into the ibex's stomach, which is rolled in flour and kept shaded. This food is kept cool and edible for up to four months. Bones are broken for access to marrow. Hides are used for tote-bags or other furnishings; horns, for knife handles. Killing for sport is unknown. Despite the hunter's pleasure after a successful kill, he praises the animal's beauty and hardiness and thanks God for this gift.

Cultivation

The desert Ma'aza do not despise agriculture, only agriculturalists. Growing crops is another nonpastoral opportunity the nomads take advantage of whenever possible. They cannot sow crops randomly, but must prepare special garden plots which they can tend only if rain falls on them. A shortage of suitable topography and rainfall prevents agriculture from having a significant, regular place in their economy.

With rain as spotty and brief as it is, there are seldom opportunities to cultivate in a given location. The garden of 'Ali 'Awaad and 'Abd al-Dhaahir Sulimaan at Umm Tinaydhab, for example, was cultivated in 1978 and did not receive rain again until 1988. A rare combination of topographic features defines a good garden site. The plot must be a depression adjacent to a major wadi bed, so that floodwaters can be diverted into the basin (*nag'aa*). Several locations like this exist in the drainages of Wadi Gattaar, Wadi al-Ghuzaa, and Wadi Abul Hassan. Over the past century, Khushmaan men have dug channels and built rock diversion dams (*jisr*) to exploit these sites, which are maintained and used by their sons and grandsons. Typically, the basin is saturated only once by a brief rainfall, immediately after which men plant crops. There is no opportunity for further irrigation.

Remarkably, a single spring rain is sufficient to produce one autumn harvest of some especially hardy crops. Most often planted are barley, millet, maize, watermelon, Malta jute, sweet melon, snake cucumber, and okra. Winter crops include chick peas, Egyptian lupine, lentils, fava beans, and fenugreek. Bedouins on the South Galala Plateau also cultivate a variety of tobacco renowned for its potency. Growers and their families consume most of their harvest, although sometimes they are able to sell a surplus; for example, Muhammad Umbaarak in 1983 sold about two hundred watermelons he had grown at Wadi Abul Hassan to passersby on the Qena-Safaga road, earning $165 (130 £E). The nomads enjoy such ephemeral farming. Rainfall that allows for a crop also produces localized pasture for livestock. This means the entire family is together, with women and children tending sheep and goats nearby while men work the field and entertain visitors.

The Bedouins undertake a second, less common form of cultivation at permanent water sites. Typically the growers are older men like Naafil Saliim in the 1960s and Suwaylim ʿAwaad in the 1980s whose grown children look after them. Naafil Saliim settled at Bir Umm Anfiiʿa for eight years, irrigating apricots, tomatoes, Malta jute, and dates until his death in 1971. Nothing remains today but the ditches he dug and some makeshift palm frond fences. Suwaylim ʿAwaad is famous for his green thumb and enjoys transplanting many local perennial trees and shrubs, including crown-of-thorns tree, wild fig, acacia, ben-tree, retam, argel, and wormwood; and exotics like the castor-oil plant, pomegranate, aroquette, Indian mallow, coriander, and tomatoes. Suwaylim even asked me to bring him seeds of coffee and cardamom which, unlike the seeds he had tried, would grow successfully. He proudly tended a garden near the Qena-Safaga road for more than a year, finally abandoning it in disgust after motorists repeatedly stole his tools. In 1986 he found a haven at the remote well of al-ʿAyn where he planted his most elaborate garden yet.

Water

Water is the nomad's most important resource. The Khushmaan regard their homeland as exceptionally well endowed with this precious commodity. It is, but only in comparison with even more desiccated surrounding areas. For their poverty of water resources, the Bedouins have a surprisingly rich vocabulary for water supplies, based on such characteristics as topography, rates of flow, accessibility, reliability, and taste.

To the Maʿaza the finest water source is the "dripping place" (*naggaat*), represented in their territory by only two sites. The droplets for which these places are named fall ceaselessly from cliffs to irrigate maidenhair ferns, mosses, and reeds which, after a heavy rain, may be broken and twisted by the weight of falling water. These drippings feed permanent, shaded pools of water to which ibex, birds, and people come regularly. The nomads say that the water of these places is "like sugar, sweeter than the Nile's." In contrast are the waters they say are "more bitter than colocynth gourd," including the supply of the town of Ras Gharib and of some wells in the interior.

The Khushmaan have few wells, but they sometimes dig a new one or excavate an ancient well. Some date from Roman times. One of these, Bir Gattaar, is so deep at an estimated 165 feet (50 m) that the Bedouins, lacking sufficient rope, are unable to use it. Ma'aza men dig wells with rudimentary, usually makeshift tools. The procedure is laborious and time-consuming and often ends in disappointment. The great Khushmaan "engineer" 'Awaad Saliim dug a one-hundred-foot (30 m) well at the junction of Wadis Gattaar and al-Atrash, but failed to find water. Saalih began digging a well in Wadi Umm Haadh in 1982 and finally in 1988 reached water at fifty-five feet (17 m). It was saline and of no value. At some wells the Bedouins have built functioning windlasses, and at others they improvise to reach water. At Bir al-Kraym I saw a six-year-old boy lowered repeatedly on a sixty-five-foot (20 m) rope to fill a discarded tire that served as a bucket.

A greater portion of the nomad's permanent water supply comes from surface water than from wells. Some, such as the camels' water at Araas, are open-air sources (*shiri'a*). Another permanent supply is the gravel seep from which a man must scrape away sand to expose the precious liquid. The Arabs distinguish three varieties of seeps: the *thamiila*, which refills promptly; the *irsays*, which yields little water and recharges slowly; and the *umshaash*, which delivers even less. A rarer permanent surface water source is the spring (*'ayn*), with Umm 'Anab and Gattaar Abu Tarfa the only examples in the entire Khushmaan territory.

The Arabs' most anomalous permanent water is Shatuun, in the limestone country. They marvel at its volume and apparent independence from rainfall, despite its resemblance to a rock basin. The pool occupies a 140-foot (43 m) stretch on the floor of Wadi Shatuun, at the base of a 30-foot (9 m) narrow, 70-foot (21 m) high defile. Visiting Shatuun after a seven-year drought, Thomas Russell calculated its contents at 46,000 gallons (1949, 109). Swimming the length of the Shatuun water (a first, my guides assured me), I submerged to its maximum depth at twenty-three feet (7 m). Von Dumreicher's guides told him Shatuun would go dry after twelve rainless years; my Ma'aza companions insisted this would never happen (1931, 141). Some believe it is connected directly with the Nile, thirty-seven miles (60 km) away, because in the old days when the Nile flooded people saw Shatuun rise, only to subside when the river was low. The Khushmaan generally avoid Shatuun because of frequent visits there by ruthless Mutayr tribesmen and prefer when possible to use the impermanent Shifawiyya water thirty-seven miles (60 km) to the northeast, which they say the Mutayr do not know about.

Rain-fed rock basins fulfill more of the nomads' watering needs than do wells and springs. The Bedouins call these *galt, masak, kharaza,* or *makra'*, according to the topography where they occur, their volume, rate of evaporation, and accessibility for livestock. Some basins retain water for only a few days; some, for several years. Knowing how long a given basin holds water and when it last received rain is standard lore, as misinformation may mean death. As basins are replenished only by rainfall, people use them very conservatively. For example, while the nomads bathe lavishly at wells, they splash themselves only lightly at rock pools. Some of these basins are in very difficult to reach locations and require long hikes over rocky terrain. Carrying water to camels and other livestock from such sites is one of the Bedouins' most demanding labors. Ironically, water is sometimes a killer in the Maʿaza desert. Several Bedouins have fallen into and drowned in water basins which lie at the feet of steep cliffs.

The short-lived phenomenon of abundant runoff after a great rainfall is one of the nomads' greatest joys. When we reached massive pools in Wadi Naggaat following a downpour, Saalih gleefully asked me whether he should drink from this one, or would that one be better. Kneeling, he drank directly from the surface of a fine pool.

Leo Tregenza (right) with the author at Land's End.

The nomad's "dreamscape," a wadi full of green plants;
here, *silli* (*Zilla spinosa*), Graygar.

Before inundation of a basin
in Wadi Abu Nakhayla,
South Galala Plateau.

After inundation of a basin in
Wadi Abu Nakhayla, South Galala Plateau.

A man's *sufun* containing necessary items; note the plastic sandal.

Saalih ʿAli at the end of a chase, Wadi Abu Shayba;
the young ibex would be introduced into his herd to be reared "as a goat."

Shaking *Acacia raddiana* leaves with a camel staff to feed livestock, Wadi Umm Dhaayih.

A hyrax (*wabr, Procavia capensis*), captured briefly for this photograph and released, Wadi Umm Haadh.

A sheep and a *salaaga* dog, Wadi al-Merkh.

Suwayri of the Duwaasha clan with a donkey replacing a camel he had lost, and a camel, Wadi Abu ʿAbiid; the bags are full of wormwood and argel.

Saalim Silmi (left) and others watering camels at Bir al-Kraym; note the working windlass.

Sulimaan Mara'i (left) and Sulimaan Saalih harvesting wormwood (*Artemisia judaica*), Wadi Haamid.

Sulimaan Maraʿi and camel, Wadi Abu ʿAbiid.

An ancient trap (*nusrit adh-dhiib*) for leopards and other wild predators, with Sulimaan Saalih, Wadi Naggaat.

Harvest of ben-seeds (of *Moringa peregrina*),
Wadi al-Radda.

A two-year-old male ibex captured by men and a dog
in Wadi ʿAdayd, South Galala Plateau.

Rear of a wool house, Wadi Umm Ishgilaat.

Final moments in a rare foot chase of a gazelle, Wadi Dhuwi;
in the summer persistent hunters, with weapons of rocks and a good supply
of water, can outlast their quarry.

A viper hidden in the sand, Wadi Abu Nakhayla;
Sulimaan Saalih had told me, "Don't sit there; there's a viper,"
but I did not see the animal even when I took this photograph.

Then Sulimaan put a stick to the viper's head,
and its location was revealed; he killed the animal.

Muhammad Umbaarak,
Wadi ash-Shifawiyya.

An eyed dabb-lizard (*dhabb, Uromastyx ocellatus*), Bir al-Kraym.

Yasar (*Moringa peregrina*) tree, Wadi Naggaat.

Crown of thorns trees (*sidr, Zizyphus spina-Christi*)
at the Roman way station of Dayr Umm Sidr.

Jebel Shaayib al-Banaat (uppermost) from the summit of Jebel Kuhila.

ʿAdayd Canyon, one of the largest gorges in the South Galala Plateau; the tree is a wild fig (*Ficus pseudocyomorous*).

A juvenile ibex and the goat herd into which it was introduced,
on the coastal plain near Jebel Ghaarib; the wild animal suckled from a goat
which had its own young.

Sulimaan ʿAwda and his wife, Nuwayjaʿ, toward the end of his desert career;
near the Qena-Safaga road.

A woman making *fatiira*, a bread fried on sheet metal, Wadi al-Markh.

Signatures (*wasm*s) of the Khushmaan (resembling the letter H), Hamadiyiin, Shuhbaan, and Tababna clans of the Maʿaza tribe; scrawled on a rock in Wadi Abu Nakhayla.

Muhammad Umbaarak's millet garden in Wadi Abul Hassan.

The gravel seep (*thamiila*) of Miraatba in upper Wadi Haamid;
note plastic jerrycan.

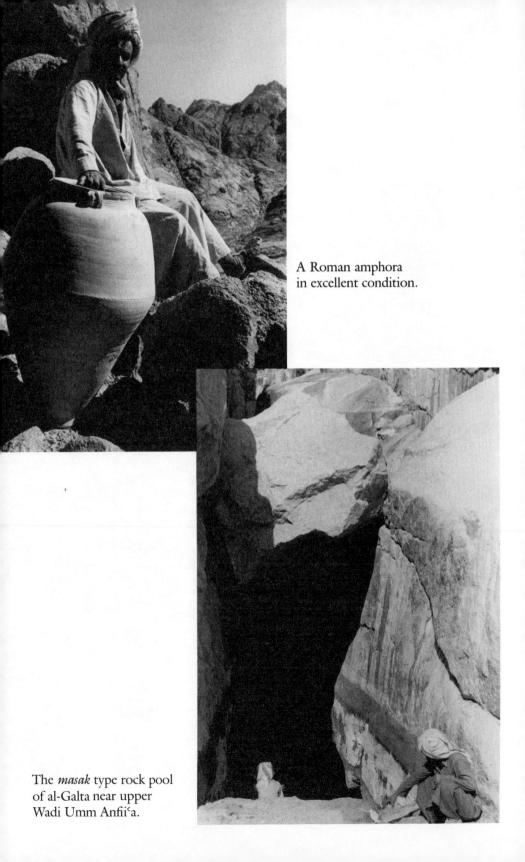

A Roman amphora
in excellent condition.

The *masak* type rock pool
of al-Galta near upper
Wadi Umm Anfiiᶜa.

The acacia preserve of ʿAwda Umbaarak at Umm Yasaar;
there is a single *Moringa peregrina* tree at the lower right.

A truck carrying American wheat from Safaga to Qena; Khushmaan women
are feeding their goat herd on wheat spilled along the roadside.

Camels, South Galala Plateau.

The Khushmaan cemetery at Umm Anfiŕa,
with the peaks of Umm Araaka in the background.

Aerial view of the Labyrinth or Maʿaza Limestone Plateau,
looking east from over the Nile Valley toward Jebel Ghaarib.

4. Belongings and Beliefs

His duties as Khushmaan *shaykh* had kept Musallim Sulimaan in the town of Hurghada for several weeks. Now that we were at Umm Sidr in the high country, Musallim was pleased to be relieved of the anxieties of city life and was exuberant about the freedoms of Bedouin life. He told me this proverb: "The material things of this world defer to God. The good fortunes they bring are pleasant, and the distress they cause are temporary."[1] The nomads take pride in the material simplicity of desert life and the good physical and mental health it engenders. "You can't take it with you" is a maxim they live by. Such virtues, along with the comforts and continuities that Islam and folk beliefs provide these pious people, help make the desert a secure home for the Khushmaan.

Material Culture

The nomads' is a world of bone, hide, hair, wood, and stone. When Bedouins break camp, there is no waste of cans, papers, and plastic, but only things they have taken from the landscape and modified to suit their needs. These materials may be arranged somewhat differently than they were long ago, but they perform the same functions.

The archeology of nomadism is largely a study of how people have handled stones. The Arabs themselves enjoy examining an abandoned camp (*daar*) of their predecessors. Typically this is a semicircle of stones that had been placed to secure the fringe of a wool tent and remained when camp was broken. In some spots there are traces of the camps of ten or more families. Those were the good days, the nomads say, when pasture was more plentiful and there was plenty of goat's and camel's milk.

Ma'aza "archeologists" can distinguish whether these were campsites of their own ancestors or those of the 'Ababda. The 'Ababda used several small stones (*mardhuufa*) for making bread, whereas the Ma'aza made their bread on a single stone (*tabuuna*). The *mardhuufa* was a circle about eight inches (20 cm) across, composed of small stones. The cook lit a fire on top and let it burn to glowing coals. He removed the embers and placed his millet dough on the hot rocks, then pushed the coals back on top of the dough. In the Ma'aza *tabuuna* technique, the cook placed a flat stone atop three support stones and lit a fire below. When its undersurface became very hot, he flipped the stone and poured dough on top. He then turned the stone over again, with the dough adhering to it and facing the hot coals. Finally, he buried the entire oven in sand for about an hour to bake the bread. The Ma'aza used this method until the 1950s, when processed wheat flour became available. Since then men have prepared *gurs*, a pizza-like dough of flour, water, and salt baked directly between the sand and a layer of hot coals. Women make another bread (*fatiir*) by frying a tortilla-like dough on a piece of sheet metal. *Gurs* or *fatiir* dipped in a thick soup of lentils (*'ads*) or Malta jute (*mulukhiyya*) is the Bedouin's most common meal.

The Ma'aza and 'Ababda used different types of stone ovens for cooking ibex, gazelle, sheep, or goat meat. The Ma'aza *zarb al-laham* was a modification of the *tabuuna,* and the 'Ababda *saltuut,* a variation of the *mardhuufa.* Once glowing coals were set in the *zarb al-laham,* sliced meat was piled on them. The stone roof was not overturned; instead, small stones were chinked to provide a complete enclosure around the meat, and this was buried in sand. After twelve to twenty-four hours, the meal was ready. The 'Ababda *saltuut* simply required larger rocks than its bread-making counterpart. The 'Ababda and Ma'aza alike used copper pots for the first time in the 1940s. In the 1960s they took to aluminum, and traditional meat ovens fell out of regular use.

Traditional household necessities made of stone also included a mill-stone (*arhi*) for grinding millet; a raised platform of rocks (*wafadh*) to protect food and other belongings from hot sand, ants, and other vermin; prop-stones (*hifaayidh*) for a cooking pot; and a rock enclosure to shelter young livestock at night against predators (*zarb al-baham*).

The Bedouins use rocks to communicate. Austin Kennett, an English explorer of the Western Desert, wrote that the Bedouins there had a complete language of cairns, some of which told jokes (1925, 89). Ma'aza rock language is not this sophisticated, but it is essential for survival. Routes to water are always marked carefully with stones at short intervals so that a child or lost adult can find the way. Similarly, over the years Bedouin walkers have marked the best trails to take through difficult mountain terrain. In former times when people cut trees for charcoal, a stone set on top of a stump meant "Don't dig out the roots, I'm coming back for them."

Wool, hide, bone, and horn satisfy many of the nomad's needs, as might be expected in a culture where wild and domestic animals have such a prominent role. The classic Bedouin black tent, or "wool house" (*bayt ash-*

sha'ar), is made of goat wool or a blend of goat and sheep wool. Some twenty-five feet long by twelve wide (8 × 4 m), it is always pitched to face the rising sun, providing maximum protection against the prevailing north winds and the heat of the afternoon. It is divided into two sections: that for men, the *sh'ig*, on the right as you face the tent; and the *muharram*, the "forbidden place" for women, on the left.

The waterskin (*girba*) was until recently the Arab's most important belonging. There are two kinds, "polished" (*swaykniyya*) and "original Bedouin" (*'arabiyya*). The former is a tanned and oiled ibex, gazelle, or goat skin (previously also Barbary sheep skin), turned inside out so that the formerly hairy surface is in contact with water. It normally lasts two to three years, but Muhammad Umbaarak swore by his *swaykniyya*, insisting that with minor repairs it would last seven years. Camels prefer waterskins to the rigid plastic jerrycans now in fashion, he added. Although it does not keep water as cool as the *'arabiyya* does, covering this skin with a specially fitted loose cloth cover (*firaash al-girba*) prevents overheating. The "original" *'arabiyya* is a tanned but unoiled goat skin which cools its contents by evaporation. The skin is not inverted. Some water must be kept in it at all times or it will become brittle and fracture. Its usefulness usually does not exceed a year.

Animal products supply many other tools. Camel wool is used in the warm caps (*tagiyya*) that many men wear and, ironically, is spun into the camel hobble (*'agaal*). Gazelle hides are fashioned into totes for sugar and flour (*jiraab*). The skin of a young gazelle, ibex, or goat serves as a milk container which is essentially a small version of the *swaykniyya* waterskin. A female gazelle's horn makes a fine holder (*mirwida*) for powdered antimony (*kuhl*), which is used cosmetically and to treat eye infections. The horn doubles as a device (*mis'ad*) to move weft thread on a loom.

Plant materials furnish many tools and amenities.[2] Dead vegetation or standing plants make up the windscreen (*hadhiira*), a sleeping shelter that the Khushmaan widely prefer to the wool house. In Wadi Bali, Saalih gloated over his choice of campsite, a large clump of toothbrush trees. The intricate limb network and prolific foliage of this plant provide a fine barrier against the elements. "Look, it's like a tent, good for sleeping. And with winter here, the vipers are gone. Our tent even gives us firewood!" A windscreen has the advantage of being readily available and dispensable. There is none of the inconvenience of toting around a huge wool house. But there are drawbacks. On cold winter nights, the windscreen is often inadequate. The Arabs sleep fitfully and wake regularly to rekindle fires and warm themselves. They sit like stones, talking only a little, absorbing enough warmth to hold them in sleep for a while longer. The Arabs almost always retire at nightfall, and winter nights are long enough that they usually wake up rested. Their beds are depressions (*garmuus*) scraped in soft sand (*budhaa*) or gravel to reduce exposure to the wind. In rocky terrain they excavate small shelters or use natural caves as sleeping places.

Branches of acacia, wild fig, and ben-tree give the Arabs the "columns" (*al-ʿawamiid*) for their wool houses. A straight limb of an acacia tree makes an excellent camel staff (*mahjan*) which doubles as a stick to shake down acacia leaves and seed pods to feed livestock. A hollowed-out ben-tree limb makes a fine storage container (*hugg*) for the small coffee cups used on formal occasions. Ben-tree bark (*ghaylda*) provides a red waterfast dye for clothing, and ben-seeds yield a fine cooking oil (*samna*). Before aluminum pots appeared, the Arabs used bowls (*hinaaba*) made of tamarisk wood; old timers like Sulimaan Maraʿi still do. Woods of acacia and *tundhub* (*Capparis decidua*) are preferred for camel saddles.

Local plants supply tannins for waterskins and for sheepskin carpets. Acacia bark (*najub*) is particularly useful. To cure the sheepskin, the bark is boiled and cooled. The skin is staked out wet, hair down, and this liquid poured on it a few times over several days. When dried, this mattress is ready for people to use. The bark of acacia, *butm* (*Pistacia kninjuk*), and ʿ*irn* (*Rhus tripartita*) and acacia seed pods traditionally provided tannins (*dabagh*) for waterskins. The woody material was broken up and boiled in water. The waterskin was left to soak in this solution for three or four days and was sometimes imbued with red ben-tree dye.

When leaving camp for a few days or weeks, the nomads store and protect their belongings (*wahad*) by hanging them in the branches of an acacia or other tall tree or suspending them from a tripod built of tree limbs (*muʿallag*). It would be an unacceptable breach of desert ethics for anyone to pilfer these stores. The Khushmaan today tell the story of a man named Salaama whose *wahad* was violated. Angry, he was careful to hide his next storehouse. He died and it was never found. Perhaps, they say, there is money or sugar in it.

Edible plants include the caper (*lassaf, Capparis cartilaginea*), a close relative of the pickled variety available in the West. Preferring the pulp over the seeds, the Bedouins eat capers as they ripen on the lower mountain slopes in late summer and fall. They also make a kind of liquid "fruit-cake" (*mariida*), throwing fifteen to twenty dried caper fruits (*jaru*) into a pot of boiling water, adding a bit of flour and goat's milk, and storing it for up to two months in the *swaykniyya* waterskin. The result is, one man said, "like milk, but a little spicy, good tasting and good for you." A few fruits cooked with salt and vegetable oil, then cooled and applied to affected areas, help ease the pain of rheumatism.

Wild figs (*Ficus pseudosycomorous*) ripen in the mountains in late summer and despite their small size are delightfully sweet. After picking them the Arabs are careful to let the fruits sit for at least a half-hour before eating them. This reduces the effect of an irritating chemical in their latex. Fig trees are not common enough to be commercially important. However, the Bedouins, young men in particular, often climb a mountain just to enjoy a few handfuls.

Dates are a favorite but uncommon food. Men have planted date palms in the only suitable locales, the water sources of Jebel Gattaar, Wadi Umm Anfiiʻa, Wadi Qena, and Wadi al-Mallaaha. These palms are living epitaphs of grandfathers and great-grandfathers. In principle only the planter's direct descendants may harvest a particular tree's dates, but in practice any passerby may help himself to a few, while the heir is entitled to the lion's share.

The Khushmaan have experimented with many plants they thought might be edible, with mixed results. While *huwwi* (*Launaea nudicaulis*) is delicious fare, its close relative "dog's ass *huwwi*" (*huwwi tiiz al-kalba, Reichardia tingitana*) is inedible; so is the "dog plant" (*dharamit al-kalb*), which one man described as tasting "like blood in your mouth when you have a bloody nose." One success was wild orache (*gataf, Atriplex leucoclada*), a plant which flourishes in limestone areas and tastes like salty cheese. The seed pods of *markh* (*Leptadenia pyrotechnica*) are edible but flavorless. The nomads eat the seeds but not the pulp of *tundhub* (*Capparis decidua*). In hard times the nomads eat acacia gum (*samgh*).

Experimentation with plants has yielded other notable uses. Spider flower (*mashta, Cleome droserifolia*) ingested as a tea suppresses coughs and moderates the burning effects of botfly larvae in the mouth. Rubbed in the hair or mustache, its leaves make a pleasant "cologne." Before soap could be purchased readily, people made it from leaves of *gilu* (*Anabasis setifera*) and *rutrayt* (*Zygophyllum coccineum*). The Arabs still fashion camel hobbles from palm fiber (*liif*). Plants also provide fuel for the traditional flint-and-steel fire starter. A small piece of old cloth is imbued with the powdered foliage of argel, *girayʻa* (*Papaver decaisnei*), or *jithaath* (*Francoeria crispa*). Dried colocynth gourd, ben-tree needles (*haruut*), camel dung, and even hair from a sheep's chin (*wadah an-naʻaaj*) also make good tinder. The fuel is placed on a piece of flint which is struck with a steel ring (*zinaad*) or a knife blade to spark a fire.

Campfires have tremendous practical and cultural importance. The Arab will not eat without bread, which only fire provides. Fire boils the tea that relieves the strain of physical labor, brings people together, and stimulates social intercourse. Drinking tea and conversing around the fire is the Bedouins' principal entertainment. Collecting fuel is the first chore in a new camp. Usually it is dead roots and branches of *Zilla spinosa, Leptadenia pyrotechnica, Moringa peregrina,* and plants of the wadi floors and mountain slopes. Larger limbs are smashed with great rocks. One man explained why this task is despised in mountainous areas: "the botfly hears this and thinks it is the sound of horns of sparring ibex. She comes to you and not finding her preferred victim sprays her stream of maggots into your eyes and mouth."

Perhaps the greatest revolution in Bedouin material culture occurred about 1970 with the introduction of the plastic jerrycan (*jarrican*). Inexpensive and durable, it has largely replaced the waterskin, and with some cloth and cord can be made almost as comfortable for transport by camel and man. If you drop a waterskin, the Arabs note, it will break open and your precious water will be lost; but the jerrycan will not break.

Bedouin footwear has also undergone changes. Until this century people made their own sandals from gazelle hide, and a few men like Musallim Sulimaan still do. At mid century the Arabs began to fashion sandals from discarded tires. These were more durable, lasting up to a year, but are almost obsolete now. People prefer the open plastic sandals, manufactured in Hong Kong, which cost about $1.90 (1.50 £E). These begin to split apart after about three months, but their resourceful owners patch them for up to a year by fusing on pieces of discarded sandals. In the granite country I wore out three pairs of French and American boots before Saalih gave up on a single pair of flimsy plastic sandals. He once moved up to a pair of closed sandals costing $15 (12 £E). They were in shreds after a week, so he went back to the original model.

Automobiles were just being introduced into Khushmaan life in the 1980s. Four men owned small Japanese pickup trucks by 1988. These entrepreneurs, whose households are in the Red Sea and Nile towns, are the middlemen who buy desert produce of livestock, ben-seeds, and wormwood from their kinsmen and transport such cargo to market. Bedouins who have experience with automobiles have developed characteristically ingenious ways of maintaining them with materials at hand. Saalih and I drove an old Toyota on a long haul from the Khushmaan homeland to the South Galala Plateau. In upper Wadi at-Tarfa, a desolate plain of sharp limestone, we blew out one tire and then our only spare. In this waterless district, there was no chance that we could walk to safety. The only option was to fix a tire, but we had no repair kit. Saalih envisioned a most unlikely solution. Our best spent tube had a four-inch gash. He bunched the rubber around this tear like the skin of an accordion and punched a steel nail through the folds as I watched in dismay. Around this he wrapped a piece of cloth torn from his headscarf. He secured this "patch" by tying my leather shoelace tightly around the nail. We inflated the tire and drove nervously sixty-eight miles (110 km) into Ras Gharib.

Radios appeared in the 1960s and are now in about half of the desert households. Musallim Sulimaan was the first to have one. "It was clumsy and required a separate antenna and battery," he recalled. "At first people were amazed and would gather around it, like they do around a television when they visit town now. Soon there were many, and you could take them anywhere." Arabic services of the BBC, VOA, and Monte Carlo bring incongruous information to the Eastern Desert. Radios reaffirm the nomads' perception that settled people are foolish. In the winter of 1984 they quizzed me about the toys that were so important that Americans spent hours queued up in the cold to buy them: Cabbage-Patch dolls. Sometimes the information is both strange and unpleasant: "What is a nuclear weapon?" several people asked me.

One expression of the nomads' conservatism is their adherence to time-honored methods and materials. Another is their rejection of the gadgets of settled life that they regard as unnecessary or harmful. They believe that some technologies cause people to do things they were not meant to do. While curious about the power source and speed of aircraft, for instance, the Bedouins do not wish to fly. Saalih could not imagine anything worse: in a crash, he said, three hundred or four hundred people perish and are spread across the ground "like tomatoes." He himself had survived an equally improbable accident by clinging to a friend's capsized fishing boat in the Red Sea. "Between man and the sea or sky," he concluded, "there can be no mutual understanding."

Values, Religion, and Ritual

Their material possessions have an important effect on the Bedouins' values and beliefs. In just a few minutes a Khushmaan family can break camp and pack everything they own on a single camel. The ideological significance of having few belongings but great mobility is especially well developed. The nomads believe that their abilities to make use of things at hand distinguish them from settled people, who rely on others to provide for them. Some fear that this sense of personal resourcefulness is waning:

> In the old days people weren't lazy. In the old days people climbed mountains to fetch *'irn* to cure their waterskins. They ground millet by hand in their millstones. They made garments from cloth they bought in market. When these got too worn to wear, they made blankets of many colors from them. They wove great wool houses. People are lazy now and don't make wool houses. Before, people made waterskins from ibex or gazelle, instead of using jerrycans. Now they buy flour instead of grinding grain. They are getting more lazy. Years from now you will find them staying by water all the time!

Despite such laments there has been little real change in Bedouin technology, even among the younger people. Certain materials have been substituted—plastic for animal hide and machine-made for hand-made clothing—but basic functions remain the same. These changes, even the use of radios, have not altered significantly the Khushmaan view of the world and their special place in it.

Freedom

Having freedom (*al-hurriyya*), which they insist only a desert life permits, is the Bedouins' most esteemed value. They are reluctant to spend much time at any one place, regardless of profit. The choice between leading a relatively prosperous sedentary life and a mobile one was posed in a conversation Saalih and I had at the well of Umm Anfiiʿa. He began:

> Yaa Salaam! If only you had a drill, you could put twenty wells here. You could plant palms, figs, lemons, pomegranates, and oranges, and build a house, and stay at the garden.
> ["Who would stay at the garden, you?" I asked.]
> Not me! I always have to see what is going on in Wadi al-Ghuzaa, or in Wadi Umm Anfiiʿa. I must always move. To stay here, or in any one place, would be like prison.

There is a large repertory of Khushmaan stories about Bedouins who escape figurative or real prisons for the freedom of the desert. One story relates how government officials ordered some people of the Tuwaara tribe to move from the Red Sea Province to a new settlement at Wadi al-Jadiid in the Western Desert. One intractable tribesman did not want to lose his freedom, so he fled Hurghada on foot before sunset, passed through Wadi Bali, Wadi al-Mallaaha, and Wadi ad-Dibb, and reached Bir Daara at sunrise. He had covered seventy-one miles (115 km) in a fourteen-hour freedom flight.

Although the Maʿaza regard the Howeitat as traditional enemies, in this account they admire them for valuing freedom:

> There were two Howeitat prisoners laboring at the Tura limestone quarry near Cairo. One had twenty years remaining on his sentence, the other six days. One day while they worked in the quarry the man who had six days left hid the man who had twenty years left—ball, chain, and all—among some boulders. That night the hidden man was able to remove the boulders and drag himself four kilometers or more into the desert, where some of his people were camped. They released him from his shackles, and together they fled. They were joined after a few days by the other prisoner when he completed his sentence.

The Khushmaan believe their homeland has always been a landscape of freedom. One historical figure in their folklore is a man they call Bayduunis. He was actually Poseidonius, a Christian anchorite whose story is told in a fourth-century text. Somewhere near Mons Porphyrites (Jebel Abu

Dukhaan), site of the Roman quarry for Imperial porphyry, he sought refuge from Roman soldiers, for if apprehended he might have been enslaved. He described his life as a fugitive:

> I have not spoken to a man for a whole year, and I have not heard the speech of one. I have not eaten bread, but the insides of palm leaves soaked in water and, whenever I could find it, wild honey. Once, however, the time came when these things failed me, and I was in sore tribulation because of it. And I went forth from the cave that I might go to the habitations of men, and having journeyed on the whole day I was scarcely two miles distant from the cave. And I turned [and looked] behind me, and I saw, as it were, a horseman whose appearance resembled that of a knight, and he had upon his head the similitude of a helmet, and thinking that he was a Roman I turned back to the cave. (Budge 1907, 1:173–174)

Having read this account, Leo Tregenza surmised that Poseidonius's refuge might have been the Christian hermitage at Wadi Naggaat, near Jebel Abu Dukhaan. The Khushaymi Sulimaan Suwaylim guided Tregenza there, and the two men found an inscribed stone near the church. Tregenza later translated the inscription, which had nothing to do with Poseidonius. Apparently, however, Tregenza told Sulimaan Suwaylim the story of Poseidonius, and the Khushaymi thought it was this story that had been recorded in stone at Naggaat. Consequently, Bayduunis has become a folk hero to the modern Khushmaan. He "preferred possible death to oppression" and "chose hunger over imprisonment," they say. He was like a Bedouin: "The Arabs are not like *fallaahiin,* who are like flies. The *fallaahiin* might think prison is nice, with good food and rest, but not the Arabs. We must live free. Death is better than prison, just as Bayduunis believed."

The nomads' preference for personal space differs markedly from that of sedentary people. Except on very cold winter nights, the desert Khushmaan prefer to sleep under the stars rather than be confined even under the roof of the traditional wool house. Saalih and I were the guests of an 'Ababda laborer in his concrete home at the Umm Howeitat mining village. While remaining courteous, Saalih was visibly unnerved in the confinement of the reception room. When we finally broke away and started up Wadi Jasuus, he was jubilant. "Look, I'm all water," he said: his *jalabiyya* (robe) was soaked with perspiration.

The desert Khushmaan regard the values of "bread and salt" (*aysh wa milh*)—that is, the ethics associated with sharing food—as being uniquely Bedouin. The mutual trust and assistance guaranteed by this food covenant are extremely important in interpersonal relations. Generosity and hospitality are its adjuncts. "We are the only people who really know generosity," Saalih said. "Only after offering him tea and food do we ask a stranger 'Where are you from?' He is our guest for three days, then he is on his own. Even an enemy, if he comes in peace, is welcomed. We eat bread and salt with him to assure him there is no hostility."

Islam and Superstition

Islam is often described as a religion suited to the harsh simplicity of desert life. However, Muslim rituals such as ablution before prayer and attendance of Friday prayer in mosque favor town-dwellers. By the standards of a devout urban or village Muslim, the Bedouins appear not to be very fastidious. Other than older men and women, few pray the prescribed five times daily. Only five Khushmaan men, none of them desert-dwellers, have made the pilgrimage to Mecca that should be performed by all Muslims who can afford the trip. The nomads cannot.

Prayer and pilgrimage are not adequate indicators of the nomads' spiritual life, for they are deeply religious and thank God constantly. Seeing or hearing about something fine or unusual the Bedouin exclaims, "Subhaan Allah!" or "God be praised!" Two categories of things exist, those made by man (*swayt Bani Aadam*) and those made by God (*swayt Rabbina*). The latter are always the most esteemed and include everything in Nature: mountains, water, trees, animals, and humanity itself. It took me a long time to break the habit of saying "thank you" to the nomads. "The thanks go to God" was always their reply: we help each other as a matter of course in the service of the Higher Being.

Even with their strong faith in God, the Khushmaan maintain some superstitions. They genuinely fear others' mystical powers. Musallim Sulimaan related this account: "There was once a foreigner who visited Naggaat. He wrote something on an old cup and placed it among the rocks. For a very long time no rain fell around Naggaat. A Khushaymi said, 'I remember the foreigner writing something on a cup.' The man led a party to Naggaat. They found the cup and broke it. Rain soon fell there." This story made me uneasy. If there were a drought, would I be suspect?

Another belief is that there are good and bad days on which to travel. The second day of the second Muslim lunar month is propitious, while the nineteenth day of any lunar month is unfavorable. The worst days are the three of *al-Giraan*, "The Conjunction" of the moon with the constellation Scorpio (*al-Agrab*), and Thursdays (*yawm al-khamiis*) which fall on the twenty-fifth day of the Muslim lunar month; this unfortunate combination is called *khamiis al-khamas*:

> A long time ago a man named 'Ayrayd said, "Nothing bad can happen on any one day, all are the same." An old woman told him, "No, there are bad days, especially those of *al-Giraan*." He replied, "Nothing will happen to me on those days, or on the sixteenth or the twenty-first."

"Watch out then for *khamiis al-khamas*," she warned him. He traveled anyway on such a day. He was ambushed by enemies who threw a spear through his body, fixing him to his saddle. Three days later his mount approached his camp, and the people there said to the old woman, "Look, you can see that nothing has happened to him; you were wrong." But when the camel came closer, they saw that he was dead.

Some Khushmaan superstitions are linked with places. Sulimaan Maraʿi explained that if a man falls ill at a certain spot he should sow barley or millet in a line there and recite an invocation. This prevents subsequent visitors from getting sick there.

The Khushmaan profess not to dabble in magic but believe the ʿAbabda, particularly members of the Grayjaab clan, are great sorcerers:

Once in the days of salt smuggling four or five Grayjaab men and their camels, heavily laden with salt, were descending Wadi Qena and near the Miraaza stone spotted a scout from the Frontiers Patrol. The scout saw them too and brought up his companions to where the Grayjaab had been. At that spot they found boulders where there had been none, and there were no signs of camels or men. The scout protested, "I saw them! They could not have fled! They must have become these boulders!" He jabbed a boulder with his bayonet, and blood poured forth. He and his frightened companions fled.

There are numerous accounts of an ʿAbabda *shaykh* named Afiifi, who was no ordinary man:

He had magical powers. The children of workers at the Umm Howeitat phosphate mine would follow him into the mountains, sometimes fifty of them, and somehow he would produce water and sweets for them up there. His appearance was rag-tag, and he looked like an idiot. Once the *shaykh* was hitchhiking on the road between Safaga and Hurghada. A car stopped, and the driver got out to harass him. When the driver resumed his trip, he unwillingly left the asphalt and began driving up Wadi Saagia. He was five hours late getting home. Something had forced him to leave the road. He went to find Shaykh Afiifi and told him, "I'll take you anywhere you want to go." Another time the *shaykh* was traveling by train to Qena and asked to be let off at Qift. The conducter refused and told him he must ride all the way to Qena. The *shaykh* collected his belongings, and when he was ready the train stopped by itself, and he got off. Shaykh Afiifi and his youngest son were killed by a car in Ras Gharib in 1981. The day of the accident, the *shaykh* mysteriously told some neighbors, "We are moving on today."

The Bedouins relate many tales of *afriit* (pl. *afariit*), mischievous demons who taunt men. These spirits sometimes haunt particular locales. Salaama Sulimaan reported that at night near the abandoned gold mine of Abu Zawal people have heard the clinking of metal against rock issuing from the mines. This is the work of *afariit*, Salaama argued. Several men at different times told me the following account of an apparent *afriit:* "One night Umtayr Silmi, Afrayj Sulimaan, and some other men were camped in Wadi Guurdhi, between al-Hayta and Tuur al-Askar. About half an hour after sunset they saw a large animal, the size of a water buffalo, fleeing across the wadi faster than a man can run. The next morning when they investigated they found no tracks where they had seen the animal."

Salmaan Sulimaan recounted these occurrences of *afariit* and their kindred *jinn* ("genies"):

> On his way to Qena by camel, my father was traveling up Wadi Umm Anfiiʿa. Near al-Galta he heard a child crying among the rocks. The wailing kept pace with him until he reached the pass to Graygar. A year later he was in Showak, not far from al-Galta, hunting ibex at night with a man named Naafil. They both heard the wailing. It was the same cry my father heard before. It was an *afriit*. There are many of them in the Galaala hills, and they taunt men with their owllike calls. A *jinn* haunts Umm Diisa: a silhouette of a man with long frizzy hair appears there, then vanishes.

Jinn seem exclusively to take on human form. Saalih related a similar account of a spirit on the South Galala Plateau: "An Arab approached a stone building in the Galaala. A figure with a head of whitened kinky hair emerged and threw a stone at him. The man fled and soon died. Maybe this figure was a *jinn*. Maybe all these stories are talk, I don't know. I spent eight days by myself in Wadi at-Tarfa and enjoyed them, and nothing like this happened to me." His comment reveals how important companionship is to the Arabs in the wilderness; it is a memorable and sometimes unsettling occasion when a man is by himself for any length of time.

The Arabs are not inclined to fanciful thinking, and it bothers them that unnatural things sometimes happen. Saalih told me that on the gravel plain between Wadi Abu Haadh and Wadi Fatiira he came across a Roman road, well defined by parallel stone walls. He returned later to this very spot and found no trace of the road, attributing its disappearance to *zawwaal* ("ghosts").

Health, Healing, and Dying

The Bedouins believe that their physical as well as spiritual health is much better than that of people in the Nile Valley. One man said of children who

live in the desert: "They are just like adults, much healthier in the moun-
tains. They don't get influenza, colds, or whatever sickness is in town."
The desert people tell many stories about kinspeople who have visited the
Nile Valley only to sicken and die.

The desert Khushmaan attribute their good health to living active lives
outdoors. They pride themselves on having keen senses and for using these
to maximum advantage. Their characteristically excellent eyesight is especially prized: "One morning Sulimaan ʿAwda was with Mister Kinza [Leo
Tregenza] at Abu Shaʿar. He looked and saw his camels at a place near
where the Hurghada airport is now [11 mi., 17 km, distant]. Mister Kinza
could not see the animals, and Sulimaan ʿAwda told him to try with his
binoculars and directed him where to look: 'They are there, and Muhammad ʿAwaad is moving with them.' Mr. Kinza found them in his binoculars. The camels were moving on 'white' ground, so were especially hard to
see." Perhaps because of lifelong exposure to the intense desert sunlight,
the Arab's eyesight unfortunately deteriorates steadily after he or she
reaches the age of about fifty. Their inability to see well is one of the desert
elders' greatest complaints. None of the Khushmaan has ever had glasses,
but the need is great, as Muhammad Umbaarak demonstrated when he
said he could see "perfectly" for the first time in years when he tried on my
thick prescription glasses.

The Maʿaza have small frames, but some are quite muscular. When the
nomads speak of physical power, they often remember the Duwaasha
strongman Amiira: "Once he carried two male ibex, each with four-hand
horn spans, down Wadi Abu Maʿaamil and arrived at camp ahead of his
companion who had set out with him carrying a single, smaller ibex. Later
at Jebel Faalig, Amiira bagged two large ibex and loaded them onto a
donkey. The donkey fell under the weight, so Amiira hoisted the game
onto his shoulders and tramped off."

All of the Arabs are accomplished walkers, for their daily chores of pasturing, collecting, and hunting keep them on their feet. Some nomads,
however, have distinguished themselves as hikers. One man accomplished
a remarkable feat:

> He left Qena on foot at the same time as two men riding camels. He
> asked the men whether they would carry some of his baggage, as they
> were all traveling to the same destination. They refused. He walked on
> with all his goods, all the time staying ahead of the camels. He finally
> arrived at a large encampment in Wadi Bali [80 mi., 130 km, distant].
> The host offered him coffee—they had no tea then—and asked him,
> "Where have you come from?" "Qena," the man replied. "Get out of
> here, you liar!" retorted the host. "Wait and see," said the walker,
> "someone will come and tell you this is true." Two hours later the
> riders arrived.

The Khushmaan tell that their late kinsman Sulimaan Rashiid once left Jebel Daara on foot in the morning and arrived at Bir Kufra, forty-two miles (68 km) away, in the evening. Saalih noted that it took him two days riding a camel to cover this distance.

Muhammad Umbaarak epitomized the Arabs' energy and good health. At age fifty he walked from Wadi Gattaar to Qena in three days. His peers agree that this sixty-eight-mile (110 km) journey might require five days for most men. In 1985 septuagenarian Muhammad still walked with the stride and speed of a young man. His kinsmen attributed his fine condition to a proper life-style: much exercise and a diet which included camel's and goat's milk but not processed foods. Some Khushmaan believe such physical well-being is threatened now by the quality of the foods they must buy in town:

> My father is seventy-five or eighty years old. But he won't sit: he's got to get up and go with the camels, and go after firewood and water. In the old days all we had was millet. It wasn't particularly good food, but we got on. Look at Muhammad Umbaarak now. He's got great energy. But for much of his life he ate only millet and often knew hunger. Now we get processed wheat flour. Maybe chemicals have somehow entered into it. I think the old flour ground from grain was better. In the old days there were no chemicals. Crops were grown straightaway in the earth.

The Khushmaan pride themselves for having excellent mental health and contrast themselves with people whose problems they have heard about. Saalih conceded that two Ma'aza tribespeople, a Khushmaan woman and a Tababna man, were known suicides; "I don't know why they killed themselves," he said.

The Bedouins generally live to an advanced age after surviving the perils of childhood. Foremost among these is death by snakebite. Around dusk a barefoot child cavorting around camp or collecting firewood sometimes blunders across a viper. The child's low body weight minimizes his or her chance of survival. Khushmaan treatment for snakebite relies primarily on the intervention of a *haawi* (or female *haawiyya*), a shaman whose specialty is curing snake, spider, and scorpion bites and stings. The *haawi* does not administer medicine but breathes upon the bite, sometimes applying his spit to the wound, mouth, eyes, hands, or feet while reciting incantations. After five or six days most patients recover, say the Arabs. Only certain persons are eligible to become *haawi*s. As an infant the *haawi*-to-be is visited early in the morning on three successive days by a practicing *haawi*, who gives the candidate a special drink and bestows the power upon him.

As if not to risk all on the *haawi*, or if no shaman is nearby, the Arabs

also administer "first aid," either cutting off the flesh around the area bitten or cauterizing the wound with a red-hot nail. Another option is bleeding (*hijaaba*). In this procedure a match is lit under a cup and placed on
the flesh around the wound. This creates a suction that brings blood to the
surface. The wound is then cut wider and allowed to bleed freely. Graybeards claim that another effective treatment is to apply a piece of Egyptian vulture's flesh to the bite. A poultice made from the boiled leaves
of the *muliih* plant (*Reaumuria hirtella*) is useful on snake-bitten sheep,
goats, and sometimes men. Salmaan Sulimaan explained how people first
learned of this plant's efficacy: "Long ago, a man witnessed a battle between a cobra [*aaf, Naja haje*] and monitor lizard [*waral, Varanus griseus*].
Each time it was bitten the monitor ran to a nearby *muliih* bush and
rubbed itself in it, then returned to resume battle with the snake. The witness finally uprooted this plant. The lizard, finding it missing, could not
'recharge,' and was quickly dispatched by the snake."

Scorpion stings are seldom fatal but are especially painful for children.
Parents administer an oral prophylactic to ward off the worst effects. They
bake or fry a scorpion and pulverize it together with the seeds of garden
cress (*rashaad, Lepidium sativum*), obtained in the Nile Valley. They com-
bine this with sugar and persuade their child to take a spoonful or two over
two to three consecutive days. Powdered rhinocerus horn mixed with
water and drunk is also believed to be an excellent treatment for scorpion
stings and snakebites, although apparently few people have owned or tried
this remedy.

Ordinary colds and fever are treated with salt solutions. When I had a
fever, Muhammad Umbaarak and Saalih insisted upon showering me with
hot salty water, then wrapping my head with a towel. I felt no better, but
Leo Tregenza treated in a similar manner for heatstroke enjoyed excellent
results (1955, 190). For headaches, eye and ear infections, and some internal
pains, the technique described for snakebite of bleeding by the cup is applied to the scalp or specific affected areas. Other aches, especially abdomi-
nal pains, are treated by drinking an infusion of ambergris (*ambar*), a se-
cretion of the sperm whale's intestine, in hot water; and consuming honey
melted in tea. If all else fails, cauterization with a hot number 10 nail to the
site above the internal pain is attempted.

Accidents in the wilderness are often fatal. One of the most common
and most feared is death by thirst. This death sometimes comes in ironic
circumstances when water is close at hand. In some accounts the Bedouins
imply that victims would have lived if not for flaws in judgment and
character:

There was once a family of nine members of the Billi tribe, including
an old man and some girls, who came by boat from Arabia to trade

two camels and some goats in Qena. They landed north of Hurghada near Jebel al-ʿIsh and walked up Wadi Abu Marwa. These were the days of raiding, and they were crossing the territory of their Maʿaza enemies. When they got short on water the old man said, "The Maʿaza will give us drink." But a younger man insisted, "We can't take water from the Maʿaza; they are our enemies." The young man thought there was permanent water at ash-Shifawiyya, and led his party there. They found it dry. They did not know about the permanent water of Umm Lasayfa, only thirty kilometers [19 mi.] away. So the young man set off on camel to the Araas water 100 kilometers [62 mi.] away. He died of thirst less than one kilometer above Araas. When he did not return, a second man took the other camel and made it to Araas, returning to ash-Shifawiyya with water. But by the time he arrived six more of his companions had died. Some had wandered down Wadi Guurdhi toward Araas and perished. Only one girl survived, by drinking goat's milk.

The apparent moral of this story is that the Billi people would have lived if they had observed the Bedouin code and called as guests on their enemies. Another death with a moralistic overtone was that of an illicit couple, one man and another's wife, who eloped from Hurghada and died of thirst looking for the well of Badiʿa.

Even Maʿaza people have made fatal errors in their homeland: "Around 1900 a Khushmaan woman, a relative of Hajj Umtayr, left Umm Diisa with her donkey to buy grain in Qena. The donkey was a bad animal and made like it was thirsty, refusing to go further. So she gave the donkey a lot of water. At Maʿadaat al-Rashiidi, above Araas, the donkey halted and could not be made to continue. She left the animal and tried to reach the Araas water, but died just near it. The donkey returned to Umm Diisa. All that had happened was told in the sand." There is always a narrow margin between life and death by thirst. Saalih dubbed thirst the "idiot way-fellow," a companion no one wants. This is one of the worst ways to die, the Arabs say. Your corpse becomes black. First the fox and then other animals come to eat you.

The Khushmaan approach death of old age without apparent fear. When a person becomes too old to keep up, he or she is escorted out of the mountains down to the Qena-Safaga road. Within a mile of the road, the elderly pass their last weeks or years attended constantly by spouses and children. This location allows visits by many kinspeople traveling between the interior and market towns. There is plenty of water from roadside wells, and fresh fruit and vegetables can be obtained from truckers. Life's hardships are over, and long days of affection and reminiscence mark the close of a desert career.

As news of a death spreads, people come together to raise their palms and pray the Exhortation:

Praise be to God, Lord of Creation,
The Compassionate, the Merciful,
King of Judgement Day!
You alone we worship, and to You alone
we pray for help.
Guide us to the straight path,
The path of those whom you have favoured,
Not of those who have incurred Your wrath,
Nor of those who have gone astray.[6]

Before interment, a kinsman meticulously cleans the corpse and wraps it in seven layers of cloth. A grave is dug six feet (2 m) deep and six long in an east-west direction. On the north side of the bottom of the pit an extension is excavated to accommodate the corpse, which prevents the indignity of earth falling directly on it. The body is always placed with the head to the west.

The dead should be buried as quickly as possible. However, the Arabs dislike a loved one having a lone grave and will often transport a corpse up to three days to a Khushmaan cemetery. Sometimes this is at the deceased's request. One Khushaymi who died near Jebel Daara, where there is no cemetery, asked to be buried sixty-two miles (100 km) away at the Umm Anfiiʿa graveyard. Heeding his wish, his companions laid him to rest at one of the loveliest spots in the Eastern Desert, under the sawtooth peaks of the Umm Araaka range.

Cemeteries usually are located near a permanent water source, which offers the luxury of ritual washing. This location also promotes bonds between the living and the dead. People always come to water. They refresh themselves spiritually as well as physically, paying respects to the dead by placing a few ben-tree needles or other foliage on the tomb, making sure the covering-stones are tidy, or retying a white cloth to a palm-limb grave mast.

When cemeteries are located in waterless areas, they are often furnished to refresh the traveler or pilgrim. The simplest of such graveyards offers at least one bottle of water stored among rocks. A more elaborate version, such as at the graveyard of ʿAwaad Saliim and his kin in Wadi Gattaar, is a stone resthouse supplied with many containers of water, teacups and tea, a complete coffee service including mortar and pestle, a flour sieve, rock salt, and other useful items.

The deceased is commemorated fifteen and forty days after burial. On "the Fifteen" relatives gather by the grave to eat dates and sweets and recite the Exhortation. At "the Forty" they slaughter a sheep or goat and leave some food and water on the grave. The gesture is symbolic; unlike the ancient Egyptians, the nomads do not bury the dead with earthly possessions or leave food in the belief that souls will actually use them. The dead are always spoken of reverently with the epithets *Hayy* ("He Who Still Lives") and *al-Marhuum* ("the Deceased"). The expression "I walked with so-and-so" (i.e., "I knew the deceased") is uttered with great pride.

5. The Bedouin Landscape

Values associated with the landscape strongly influence how the Bedouins use their environment, identify themselves as kinspeople, and distinguish themselves from settled folk. Their feelings about places are sometimes related to how outsiders view their territory and behave in it. It is useful, then, to consider the Ma'aza homeland from both the nomads' and others' perspectives.

The Eastern Desert and International Affairs

Although desert, Egypt east of the Nile is not barren by international strategic and economic standards. The region is adjacent to the narrow land bridge between Africa and Asia, breached since 1869 by the Suez Canal, which links the Mediterranean Sea and Atlantic Ocean with the Red Sea and Indian Ocean. Before the canal was built, goods and pilgrims to Mecca traveled the shortest routes between the Nile Valley and Red Sea, now paved as the Qift-Qoseir and Qena-Safaga roads. Ancient Egyptians were the first to develop the region's strategic potential. After 2000 B.C. they established trade relations with the land of Punt (perhaps Somalia or Yemen) and pioneered a secure and watered route across the Eastern Desert (Weigall 1909, 15). Alongside and about halfway across this trail, which is now the Qift-Qoseir road, Ramses IV (1164–1157 B.C.) had eight thousand laborers excavate the eighty-foot-deep (24 m), still-functional well of Hammamat (Robinson 1935, 125). In Roman times the 108-mile (174 km) Qift (Koptos)-Qoseir route was so important, and the perceived threat of nomadic raiders so great, that watchtowers were built at half-day intervals along the entire distance (Murray 1912, 138). The route from the port of Myos Hormos, just north of modern Hurghada, to the Nile Valley at Qena was also vital to the Romans. In the middle of the third century, the "Mouse Harbor" of Myos Hormos boomed as the receiving entrepôt of

Roman trade for cinnamon, gums, tortoiseshell, and ivory from Arabia, northeast Africa, and India (Tregenza 1955, 94). Some of the world's most important commodities regularly crossed the Eastern Desert.

Roman trade routes across the northern Eastern Desert were also used for exporting quarried stones. The Romans scoured their empire for the finest stone, finding the best porphyry on Mons Porphyrites (Jebel Abu Dukhaan) and the finest granodiorite at Mons Claudianus (Wadi Umm Hussayn), both in Khushmaan territory. These sites are close to the Red Sea. Lacking a Suez Canal, however, the Romans chose to drag their stones up to 140 miles (225 km) for up to eight days across the Eastern Desert to ships on the Nile (Weigall 1909, 110). Rome's Pantheon and Forum of Trajan, Istanbul's Hagia Sophia and Burnt Pillar, and Baalbek's Temple of the Sun are among the final repositories of this prized rock (Murray 1967, 116–123; Tregenza 1955, 51). The cargoes were enormous, as a cracked and abandoned two-hundred-ton column of granodiorite at the Mons Claudianus quarry attests. The available technology of wooden wedges, metal tools, and oxen- and camel-drawn wagons suggests to the Bedouins a superhuman determination. The nomads marvel at Roman accomplishments still etched on the landscape, most profoundly as the quarry-wagon tracks which were furrowed deeply into the gravel plain of Wadi Qena and which two thousand years have barely weathered.

The European discovery at the end of the fifteenth century of a sea route to India around Africa's Cape of Good Hope, and the opening of the Suez Canal, all but extinguished the global importance of routes across the Eastern Desert (Meigs 1966, 64). A thriving port since Roman times, Qoseir was described in 1907 as a "strange little dream town which was sinking so surely to its death" (Weigall 1909, 88). By 1900 the transdesert traffic of pilgrims to Mecca and the trade of Nile grain for Arabian camels, sheep, and goats was almost finished (Murray 1912, 138; Tregenza 1955, 71; Weigall 1909, 76). From this nadir the Red Sea towns revived quickly. The phosphate mine of Umm Howeitat, near Safaga, began operating in 1904, and another was opened near Qoseir in 1911 (Murray 1967, 88–89). Oil drilling increased on the western shore of the Gulf of Suez after 1910. In 1930 work began on a railway between Qena and Safaga that operated briefly and was dismantled after World War II.

While they now support motor vehicles and locomotives rather than camels and wagons, the Qift-Qoseir and Qena-Safaga routes are as important to Egypt today as in the past. The Red Sea towns of Qoseir, Safaga, and Hurghada have inadequate local sources of power and potable water. Power lines from the Aswan High Dam and pipes of fresh water from the Nile at Qena wind across the ninety-three-mile (150 km) route from Safaga to Qena, paralleling a paved road. The flow of goods from the Red Sea to the Nile is also vital, as almost all the imported grain that feeds Upper Egypt is transported on this road. This wheat, supplied largely by the United States since the Camp David treaty, is off-loaded at the port of Safaga and packed into large burlap sacks. These are piled and tied down on open-bed trucks that rumble west from dawn to dusk.

In earlier days the Maʿaza benefited through violence from the strategic importance of their homeland, plundering desert caravans. Today they are peaceful beneficiaries of a very different set of resources that are provided by the outside world's use of their land. As an economical measure, the burlap sacks carrying American wheat are reused until they develop very large holes. As these sacks are loaded on flatbed trucks, any grain that spills in transit is lost. With the steady traffic of trucks, each bearing a few perforated sacks, grain accumulates along the roadside. The resourceful nomads have not failed to make good use of this apparent waste.

For the Khushmaan, 1980–1985 were lean years. Very little rain fell over the Eastern Desert, and there was virtually no green fodder available for livestock. Water sources dried up. Men went to work for wages. Families would have lost many of their animals if not for the Qena-Safaga road and the timely agreement made at Camp David. Instead of selling off their animals or losing them to drought, most Khushmaan families dispersed themselves along the Qena-Safaga route, especially on the Red Sea side of the watershed, where the greatest potholes and most perilous turns are. Women and children herded goats and sheep daily, not to green pastures but to the golden line of grain on the north side of the road. They also packed handfuls of wheat in sacks to feed their camels back in camp.

In those years the Qena-Safaga water pipe had numerous leaks and had not yet been buried in its trench. The result was a constant supply of fresh water that represented another vital resource for the needy Bedouins and their livestock. There were other beneficiaries. Resident birds and migrants such as European swallows and bee-eaters watered from the leaky pipeline. Crowned and spotted sandgrouse, desert larks, brown-necked ravens, sand partridges, and trumpeter finches fed on spilled grain. Populations of these resident birds, as well as rodents such as the Egyptian spiny mouse and silky jird, along with their predators such as Rueppell's sand fox and the sand cat grew as a result of these fortunate circumstances.

This good fortune was short-lived. There are several legitimate water taps along the Qena-Safaga pipeline, but leaks have been repaired and the line buried. A railway to carry American grain and other freight from Safaga to Qena will be operational in the 1990s, and with more solid containers it is unlikely that grain will continue to fall. This fragile, ephemeral roadside ecosystem will perish, and the nomads, their livestock, and wild animals will have to cope in more traditional ways with the next drought.

The Bedouin Universe

Artifacts of world affairs roll down the Qena-Safaga road under the inquisitive scrutiny of the Khushmaan. While pleased with any circumstantial benefits that the larger world may bring them, the nomads are not complacent about their place in it. They have their own view of the cosmos but also question in detail the world views and geographical knowledge of others.

Bedouins are born geographers and students of the heavens. Spending their lives outdoors, they lack walls and roofs that obscure views of their surroundings. Their night sky lights up to inspire wonder and curiosity. Stars are most important to the Arabs as indicators of the seasons. If you see Canopus (*Is-hayl*) low on the horizon at sunset with Sirius (*al-Mirzim*) above it, they explain, this is the end of winter and beginning of summer. When you see Canopus low on the horizon below Sirius at sunrise, summer is about to end and winter begin. Sixty days after Canopus rises (in the first week of September) is the start of "rain time," with clouds, thunder, and lightning. The nomads recognize a number of other constellations, the most important being Taurus with its principal star "the Cow" (*al-Baqr*), or Aldebaran; the Big Dipper, or "the Seven" (*as-Sabaʿa*); Aquila, or "the Falcon" (*as-Saqr*); Orion (*aj-Jawzii*); Scorpio, or "the Scorpion" (*al-Aqrab*); and the Pleiades (*ath-Thrayii*). They believe that stars are smaller and closer to the earth than the moon; each is about the size of Jebel Shaayib, the largest mountain in their desert. The Bedouins asked me what the large stars are which appear, move slowly, and disappear. I presumed these were meteors, which the Maʿaza call "lost stars" (*najma taah*). Finally, I was able to identify one as a satellite.

The lunar cycle is important to the Arabs. They reckon their ritual schedule by it, as all Muslims do. More directly, it influences their daily activities, particularly in the summer when moonlit nights allow them to walk and hunt in cool temperatures. The Maʿaza still talk about the day ʿAwaad Sulimaan saw the moon on two horizons in a single day: just above sunrise and just above sunset (Tregenza 1958, 164). I wondered whether any novice in my country would have noticed such a startling event.

I said that the moon had no atmosphere. They teased me about reports that people from my country had visited that hostile place. ʿAwaad Umtayr chuckled, "I've heard there are still four or five Americans up there!" I also claimed soberly that if your weight was sixty kilograms on earth, it would be only ten kilograms on the moon. The amused reply: "Then if you weighed fifty kilograms on earth, you wouldn't weigh anything on the moon!" While scoffing at lunar landings, they accepted the *Challenger* accident as fact and knew that a woman had been aboard.

For all their skyward attention, the nomads lack folklore about unidentified flying objects and extraterrestrial beings. Few events go unexplained. An exception was a bright light that Muhammad Umbaarak saw radiating over Jebel Gattaar for about half an hour one night: "You would say there was no night," he described it. Everyone has heard about the "year of the deep-black" (*sanat adh-dhalaymii*) about a century ago, when one morning the sun just disappeared, and the stars came out. No one knows why this happened, but years and generations are still reckoned by the event.

Which turns, the earth or the sun? That was the cosmological question the Bedouins most often asked me. Musallim Sulimaan felt, as all the nomads do, that it was the sun which turned. "If the world turned, the waters of the Nile and the seas would spill over or run uphill." Their argument is convincing:

> Those who say the earth rotates are crazy. If it did, you would be praying toward Mecca to the east in the morning, to the south at midday, to the west in the afternoon. This is impossible. If the earth turned the other way [flipped over], all would be chaos. Polaris [*al-Jadi*] remains in place, and the other stars move. If the world turned, all the stars would rotate together. The world does not turn. If it did, all the stars would appear or disappear together. The sun rises to move and set on opposite sides of the earth. In the very center of the earth is Mecca, like the centerpole of a tent. God separated the earth from the heavens, and made the earth to stand in place, and the sun and stars to revolve about the earth.

In insisting that it could not rotate or turn over, they were of course referring to a flat earth, and no one doubts that the world is flat or flat-bottomed. To clarify this I asked, "Is the world a ball, or a tea tray such as that sitting before us?" "The tray." "And what is beyond the tray?" "The seas of darkness" (*al-bahr adh-dhalamaat*). Saalim Silmi called the region beyond the edge "ruination" or "desolation" (*khuraab*). There, he said, you cannot tell which way is up. "Where does this desolation end?" I asked. "There is no end to it." There was no explanation, only reference to a Higher Power: "It is written in the Koran that God laid the earth down flat, and put mountains such as Jebel Shaayib on the earth to give it balance and keep it from spilling, and supported it with pillars like those at the corners of the wool house."

ʿAbd al-Dhaahir Sulimaan had a slightly different view, one which tried to accommodate what he had heard about the earth's vast range of climates. A hubcap was his analogy for the world. "High" countries like Egypt and the Sudan, near the top, get much sunlight, while "low" America and Britain receive hardly any. "Mister Kinza [Tregenza] told my father about days in the low country when the sun shines like the moon," ʿAbd al-Dhaahir related. These low countries are unfit for human habitation, in the nomads' view. In my winter months with them, there were radio reports of great snowstorms, and I showed them photographs of this "ice"— the rare term they invoke to describe snow. The frosts and chilly winds of winter on the South Galala Plateau are the coldest conditions they know, and they were curious about how people of the low lands live with ice.

They asked me whether I thought the earth or sun moved. It was a difficult question: my purpose was to study the Bedouin world view, not change it. I chose the least disruptive explanation: "We have a theory that the earth is a sphere, and the sun revolves around it." The spherical earth had never occurred to them, and my suggestion had no influence: they rejected it.

Most of the nomads' questions dealt with earthly geographical issues, and I answered them readily. About the planet: Are there any mountains in the world higher than Jebel Shaayib? Do the same plants found on Shaayib grow on those mountains? Which way is Korea? They had seen Koreans who work for oil companies at Ras Gharib. "They all look the same," one Khushaymi commented. Where is Sweden? They know that country is where the Scania trucks which carry bauxite from Red Sea ports to the Nile Valley are made. Is Japan cold? They asked this because the car owners among them had to modify carburetors of their Japanese vehicles to prevent overheating. On this basis Russia must be very cold indeed: no such adjustments could be made on Russian vehicles, which always overheated in the desert. How large are Russia and America? Which way is London? What lands would you encounter traveling north from here? Where is Monte Carlo? This unlikely question was raised because of the shortwave radio broadcasts originating there.

The Bedouins often asked me where America is. Only rarely did I venture the answer "this way and that way," pointing in opposite directions: on a flat earth, a given point could not be reached by traveling in either of two directions. How long does it take to reach America in an airplane? Where is wheat grown there? On "black" land, like the Nile Valley, or "red" land, like the desert? The Arabs' choice of terms is remarkable: these are the same designations the ancient Egyptians used to distinguish the Nile Valley from bordering deserts. How large are agricultural plots? How many farmers work a plot? Do they work with machines or by hand? Is there a river like the Nile in America? Are the mountains like Shaayib (granite) or the Galaala (limestone)? Are there domestic goats, sheep, camels, and water buffalo? Are there ibex? Are there cities like Cairo? Are there thieves? Are there Bedouins in America? I told them about native Americans and how our ancestors had killed them. How did these Indians obtain food? Did they have livestock or agriculture? What animals did they hunt? What belongings did they have, and how did they transport them?

"Is it true that it can be nine o'clock in one place and six o'clock in another; that it can be dark in one place and light in another?" The nomads never tired of asking me variations of this question, and almost every person I met for the first time asked it. On my first meeting with Sulimaan Mara'i, Saalih begged me to tell the graybeard where the sun was now where I came from. I did, and the old man shook his head. The response to my statements about such matters was almost always "Majesty of God!" (*Subhaan Allah!*).

The Bedouins are awed by the purported size of the earth. It is difficult for them to reconcile their detailed understanding of their homeland with the vast chaos described to them. Musallim Sulimaan, bouncing his five-year-old daughter on his lap, was philosophical: "Hamda, is the world wide or narrow?" I interjected, "It is wide," and he answered, "If you are afraid, the world is narrow. If you are not, and you are free as we are, then the world is wide."

However intrigued the Bedouins are with descriptions of foreign lands, these places have little appeal to them, and some are repulsive. An exception is Arabia, the original homeland of the Ma'aza. 'Ayd Musallim, the last Egyptian Khushmaan clansman born in Arabia, told his kinspeople that Khushmaan territory in Arabia is much like that in Egypt. The pasture in Arabia is richer, he claimed, with more rainfall and more extensive tracts of acacia woodland.

The Khushmaan know that the Gulf States of Kuwait and Qatar are poor in game because men have come from these places to hunt in Khushmaan territory, and so the nomads view these countries as inferior. There is less information about Syria, Lebanon, and Israel. Lebanon is known as a mountainous country which has an auspicious link with the Ma'aza homeland: the only two specimens of the "tree of light," which restores eyesight to the blind, grow on Jebel Shaayib and a high peak in Lebanon. However, the Khushmaan abhor Lebanon as a land of violence where live "the people who do not want to live." News of fighting there comes over the radio, and the Arabs often attribute a hazy day or the sound of a distant explosion to warfare in Lebanon.

No land is more despised than the Sudan, although no Khushaymi has been there. In the Sudan there are man-eating "near-men," human cannibals, half-man half-dog *Bani Maklab,* the great black men who formerly persecuted Ma'aza salt traders, and dangerous animals. At night, the Bedouins explain, Sudanese people sleep in solidly built huts rather than outdoors. This alone prevents their being eaten by leopards, hyenas, or other carnivores. If there were a permanent population of these animals in Khushmaan territory, Saalih proposed, not only would the Arabs not sleep outside but they would all be living in towns.

There is a closer landscape of fear, replete with cannibals, miscreants, and pestilence: the Nile Valley. One nomad said, "If I were there now I would be afraid. There are thieves and hyenas. Egyptians are afraid of our land. Why? It is completely safe."

The Bedouin Homeland

In Khushmaan thinking there is no better place to live than in what they call "our land" (*bilaadna*). The noun they use here, *al-bilaad*, has several levels of meaning. The most inclusive is its connotation as "countryside," the antonym of the cultivated and domesticated Nile Valley (*ar-riif*). In English its equivalent is "desert," and in the Arabic vernacular of non-nomads it is *as-sahraa*, meaning "desert" or "desolate waste," with the derived adjectives of "desolate" and "bleak" (Wehr 1976, 504). The nomads, however, never use these "desert" words to describe their homeland: they live in the "countryside." There is also a political dimension of the term, with *Balad al-Maʿaza* referring to the tribal territory of the Maʿaza and *Balad al-Khushmaan, Balad at-Tababna,* and so forth, to respective clan territories recognized within the greater tribal area.

Politically, it is vital for nomads to know in whose land they are. This fact establishes what rights they have to use resources which occur in a given location. Every piece of ground is affiliated with a particular kinship group. The Arabs must pay constant attention not only to where they are but to the whom of place.

As tribespeople, the Maʿaza have a territory that extends from Wadi ʿAraba south to the Qift-Qoseir road. This political region is most useful in terms of intertribal and external relations, allowing the Maʿaza to express their territorial concerns to people such as Egyptians and foreigners who are not aware that political territories smaller than that of the tribe exist. The Maʿaza expect outsiders to regard all resources within the Maʿaza political territory as Maʿaza property. At this level of territorial organization, the Maʿaza have reciprocal arrangements with the neighboring ʿAbabda tribe for using resources. Members of each tribe are allowed to pasture livestock and to use water sources within the other's territory. This is a useful arrangement during years of prolonged drought when, for example, the Maʿaza are forced far southward to where rain has fallen in ʿAbabda territory or vice versa.

On a daily-life basis, affinity with desert places and responsibility for resources is associated more with clan territory than tribal territory. There are four clan territories within the Maʿaza tribal territory, those of the Tababna, Hamadiyiin, Umsayri, and Khushmaan. The Khushmaan clan territory occupies about 21,750 square miles (35,000 sq. km), or more than one-third of the entire Maʿaza territory, between the Qena-Safaga road and a line drawn roughly between Jimsa and Asyut. In the nomads' ide-

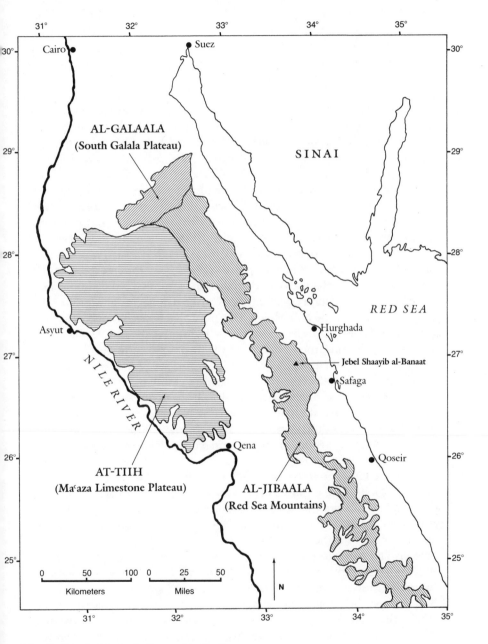

Map 5. Principal Bedouin Geographic Regions

ology, all plants and animals within the clan territory are common property of all the clan and may be used by nonclan members only with the clan's permission. Members often express this principle by marking a particular resource with the clan "signature" (*wasm*). This trademark tells members of another clan, "You are in Khushmaan territory and are using water and pasture with our permission. Be considerate in what you do here."

While tribal territory decides ownership and uses of resources between tribal or national entities, and clan territory divides these responsibilities among clans, there is no provision in the nomads' ideology for individual rights to resources in any area smaller than tribal and clan territories.

In spite of these ideals, Khushmaan lineages, families, and individuals have developed bonds with particular small areas and the natural resources which occur in them. These attachments are far more important than tribal or clan ideologies in both the Arabs' immediate decisions on how to use the environment and long-term strategies for continuing their nomadic way of life. In order to appreciate how these bonds between nomads and places have developed, it is necessary to consider another meaning of the Arabs' *al-bilaad:* the habitable or desirable landscape that is their homeland.

The habitable "countryside" of the Khushmaan begins abruptly in the west at the edge of the Nile Valley. The great Nile River is the "Sweet Sea" (*al-Bahr al-Hilw*), which has its source at "the Waterfalls" (*ash-Shallaalaat*), somewhere "beyond the Sudan." All the Bedouins know that this river flows into the Mediterranean Sea (*al-Bahr al-Abyad*), but some men were surprised when I told them it divides before emptying into the sea. The eastern border of *al-Bilaad* is the Red Sea, the "Salty Sea" (*al-Bahr al-Maliih*). Northward, the countryside ends between the Nile Delta and Suez Canal. The southern extremity of *al-Bilaad* is thought to be somewhere beyond the territory of the Bisharin tribe and the Egyptian-Sudanese border.

Within their greater countryside, the Khushmaan recognize several natural regions. One of these, the "mountainous countryside" (*al-Jibaala*) is synonymous at another level of meaning with *al-Bilaad:* it is the figurative "center of the universe," the most habitable landscape on earth. Saalih frequently called it the "Kingdom of the Arabs." It is made up of rugged igneous and metamorphic mountains representing the northern limit of the "Sudanese Alps" or "African Cordillera" which stretch southward into Ethiopia (Murray 1930, 227). The wide range of habitats these mountains provide, and their ability to create rainfall, make them an attractive home for the Bedouins. Granite rock basins hold water for months or years after rain. The best annual pasture for sheep, goats, and camels grows in the watercourses draining these mountains. The greatest concentrations of wild wormwood, ben-seeds, argel, figs, capers, and ibex and other game occur in this region. Woody trees such as acacias, which help sustain the nomads in times of drought, are most abundant in this region.

However accustomed the Khushmaan are to the grandeur of their mountain homeland, they are not oblivious to it. Each mountain has a unique personality. Each has a gender, reflecting its perceived gentle or difficult traits. Masculine Abu Harba (5,594 ft., 1,705 m) is a "hard" mountain: "it has only botflies," one Arab complained. Ghaarib (5,745 ft., 1,751 m), said another, is a "mountain of life and death: no one climbs it; it has no figs or anything anybody wants." Umm ʿAnab (5,846 ft., 1,782 m) is another "stingy" mountain: "there is barely any vegetation; ben-trees grow in only one of its drainages; there are no ibex; and its water source sometimes dries up." In contrast the Arabs regard Gattaar (up to 6,440 ft., 1,963 m), a gentle massif rather than rugged monolith, as an accommodating mountain. It figures strongly in Khushmaan geographic identity. The Bedouins have roots there: it was in the Gattaar environs that one of the founding fathers of the Egyptian Khushmaan, Sulimaan ʿAwaad Raadhi, spent his life after coming from Arabia. Gattaar boasts four permanent water sources, several fine garden sites, abundant ibex, extensive stands of acacias, and wadis full of ben-trees.

The most dominant mountain in Khushmaan life is the highest in Egypt outside Sinai: Shaayib al-Banaat (7,175 ft., 2,187 m) or, as the nomads call it, Jebel Shaayib, "Old Man Mountain." Symmetrical, lofty, and rugged, this red granite megalith has long had a special appeal to many people. Diodorus of Sicily wrote of the mountain in the first century B.C.: "Above a great plain there towers a mountain whose colour is like red ochre and dazzles the sight of those who look steadfastly upon it" (Murray 1967, 197). The Scottish cartographer George Murray described its formidable summit as "a monstrous webbed hand of seven smoothed fingers" (1967, 25).

Shaayib's honored status among the Arabs owes in part to its inhospitable character. The mountain erupts from the Red Sea coastal plain and offers no gentle slopes or easy routes. Any climb involves unshaded steep talus and dry waterfalls requiring long detours. This struggle is rewarded with breathtaking views of the Red Sea, the rugged mountains stretching from the South Galala Plateau to Qoseir, the peaks of Sinai and northwest Arabia, and the white line of humidity and smoke rising from the Nile Valley.

Although Shaayib dominates their landscape, the Arabs lack the vanities that have prompted foreigners to reach its summit, and they seldom have any reason to visit the mountain. While the mountain has game and other resources, most Bedouins regard fetching them as too difficult. One of the greatest deterrents is that Shaayib has only one permanent water source, yielding less than a half-gallon (2 liters) per day. Saalih, who probably spent more time on the mountain than most of his peers, walked on Shaayib only three times prior to our climb together in 1981. He once hiked for ten hours between the Abu 'Abiid plain at Shaayib's southern base and the upper Showak gorge on its north slope. That was in 1958, before plastic jerrycans were available, and Saalih was looking for '*irn* wood to cure his family's waterskins. He found none. In 1962 he spent four days between Umm Dhalfa and Showak gathering ben-seeds and eating wild figs. In 1972, on an unsuccessful ibex hunt, he and a companion spent a freezing night without blankets on the col between Abu 'Abiid and Showak. Examining the rock shelter that had been his campsite, we found a Neolithic rock oven, a wheel trap anchor-stone, and many flint flakes, evidence that ibex hunting had been a reason to visit Shaayib for thousands of years.

Some Bedouins who did climb Shaayib had unusual and sometimes fatal experiences which are recorded in Ma'aza folklore and place names. Most famous are the encounters two girls, the *banaat* of Shaayib al-Banaat, had with the mountain. Idrayra was an 'Ayayda girl who climbed Shaayib while her family was camped at Umm Dhalfa. From near the summit, she saw Qena, seventy-five miles (120 km) away, with her bare eyes during daylight. The nomads say this would be impossible today due to the haze produced by oilfields and warfare. Salmi, an 'Abadi, now lies buried at the base of Sidd Salmi, the precipitous dry waterfall named after her. She was walking alone, probably at night. Failing to see the danger, she fell about one hundred feet (30 m). There are several other places of death on the mountain including Hussayn's Ravine (Sh'ib Hussayn), named for an 'Abadi who was killed by a falling boulder in about 1910.

The Bedouins ascribe mystical qualities to Shaayib, believing this mountain and one other in Lebanon host the world's only two specimens of the "tree of light" (*dharamit an-nuur*). There are two reasons for the tree's name. Its leaves, applied to blind eyes, are said to restore eyesight. One Thursday night of each year, about the time ben-trees are in bloom (April and May), the tree of light gives off a luminescence that may be seen from a long distance. This may be the phenomenon that Murray's 'Ababda guides described when they told him that mysterious lights shine at night from the mountain (1967, 29).

The Khushmaan report that few people have seen the tree of light. One was a Rashayda tribesman who lived about five generations ago, the same man who reported that another specimen grew in Lebanon. As a youth he had visited the tree and collected some of its leaves. In his old age he became blind, and he rifled his residence in Qena searching vainly for the leaves. He ordered his son to travel to Shaayib and fetch him some. Just before the boy left, his father found the leaves, boiled them, and applied a few drops to his eyes. His sight was restored. Another who saw the tree was Muhammad Umbaarak's brother 'Ali, who noted that one of its larger branches had been cut with an ax long ago, perhaps in Roman times; that its leaves were like those of milkvetch (*gutbi, Astragalus vogelii*); and that its seeds resembled wheat or barley grain.

Saalih was determined that he and I should find the tree of light. He wanted me to have a specimen to share with the botanists at Cairo University. More important, he had a blind friend, a Tababna tribesman living in Ras Gharib, who would see again if we succeeded. Saalih had already tried and failed to locate the tree. Now the old man Sulimaan ʿAwda gave us specific instructions: its location could be pinpointed only from one spot at the foot of the mountain, a place called the "Mother of Fright" (Umm Jayfil). Saalih and I climbed from Umm Jayfil in December 1982, combing the slopes between the Abu ʿAbiid and Abu ʿIrn drainages where the tree should have been found. Saalih was dismayed by our failure: "The tree of light 'broke' us," he said. It never occurred to him that the tree was a myth; we would return and fail again in October 1983, only adding to the tree's mystique. Our visits to the summit while searching for the tree also revealed to the Arabs the importance that foreigners attach to the mountain. In May 1981 we found a lovely Rosenthal vase and written message left by mountaineer and entrepreneur Philip Rosenthal in 1965. In October 1983 while rebuilding the cairn that George Murray had built, we found the note Murray, his wife, Edith, and their guides signed when they finished their chore on 13 May 1943.

The Khushmaan believe that within the superior region of the "mountainous countryside," the very best area is the mountain belt from Jebel Abu Dukhaan south to the Qift-Qoseir road, encompassing Shaayib and Gattaar. Although this district is entirely within Khushmaan political territory, the nomads would deny any ethnocentrism in pinpointing the world's best landscape. They insist that God marked it as a chosen area: at the mountain place in Khushmaan territory called Abu Harba ("Father of the Lance"), He struck the granite, creating a cylindrical hole about three feet (1 m) deep.

To the Khushmaan, their clan territory stands up especially well when contrasted with neighboring desert areas. After a visit to the South Galala Plateau, my companions compared that limestone country with theirs of granite: "This is our country, where instead of dust or rock there is soft sand in the wadis for sleeping, where there are no flints flying from the fire into your eyes." The Khushmaan have difficulty navigating the plateau, which lies in Tababna clan territory some 125 miles (200 km) from the heart of Khushmaan territory. We frequently became lost on two crossings of the plateau. My dispirited and disoriented Khushmaan companions explained that the terrain is not only unknown but is difficult to learn, as there are few good landmarks. All the limestone has the same yellow shade, lacking the reds, blacks, and whites that splash their igneous country. Deep wadi floors twist unpredictably and close one in, while on the top of the 4,600-foot (1,400 m) high plateau one has the illusion of a great uncut plain and no idea where drainages lie. The Khushmaan abhor the cold winters of the South Galala: *"Bardh, mawt,"* said Muhammad Umbaarak of our January visit there: "cold, death." These Bedouins also detest the human inhabitants of the plateau and neighboring Wadi ʿAraba, even though Tababna clanspeople are members of the Maʿaza tribe. The Khushmaan perceive the Tababna as greedy and deceitful because of their excessive taste for the settled life of the Nile Valley.

The Khushmaan also dislike the metamorphic country that runs south-ward from southern Khushmaan territory into the ʿAbabda tribal area. It is hotter there, they say, because the rock is darker (my temperature records support this view). As we drank water fouled by sandgrouse at Bir Maniih, in ʿAbabda territory, Saalih claimed the ʿAbabda were short on good water whereas the Khushmaan had plenty.

The least favored of all desert areas is one which, ironically, occupies about one-half of the Khushmaan territory. Geographers know this 1,640-foot (500 m) high plateau of Eocene limestone, wedged between the Nile Valley, Wadi at-Tarfa, and Wadi Qena, as the "Maʿaza Limestone Plateau." The nomads know it as the "Labyrinth" or "Place of Straying" (*at-Tiih*) and the "Empty Quarter" (*al-Rubʿa al-Khaali*). They see it as a region of desolation, akin to what sedentary people assume is typical of deserts. Al-though its larger drainages host acacias, wormwood, and other valuable perennial trees and shrubs as well as abundant gazelles, and its heights are populated by ibex, the Khushmaan do not enforce their claim to the Laby-rinth and seldom visit the area. One deterrent is a shortage of water: the only permanent sources are in the extreme south of the area at Bir Shatuun and Umm Lasayfa. This prevents people from taking their livestock into the plateau interior, except after unusual rainfall. Also discouraging is the occasional presence of the allegedly murderous Mutayr tribesmen, who come up from the Nile Valley to harvest wormwood and hunt ibex. Some Khushmaan believe the Labyrinth is home to man-eating "near-men" (*sil ʿawi*) and therefore avoid the area. The region is also undesirable because it is topographically enigmatic: the nearly even roof of the vast plateau and its complex, sunken drainages make it truly a place of straying. My com-panions said a man might wander here for a year without encountering another person or a familiar place. It is unsettling to the Arabs to be un-aware of the names and positions of places.

Each region within the Arabs' greater countryside thus has particular physical properties and economic, historical, mythical, and social connota-tions. The combinations of these qualities distinguish some areas as better than others. A region with fine pasture and game is not good if its human occupants are despicable. The area with the best people and other attractions is the mountainous Khushmaan homeland, beyond which increasingly unknown and inferior space leads ultimately to ruination at the very edge of the earth. In the nomads' view, while they might be able to survive physically outside their homeland, that life of disorientation, rootlessness, and contact with inferior peoples would hardly be worth living.

Nomad Places and Place Making

The process by which the Khushmaan nomads have developed roots in their landscape, fashioning subjective "place" from anonymous "space," and the means by which they orient themselves and use places on a daily basis deserve special attention: these are essential parts of the Bedouins' identity and profoundly influence how they use resources and affect the desert ecosystem.

The Bedouins have little need or knowledge of maps. The Mercator projection of the world is meaningless. One evening as three of the men watched television news in Hurghada, they argued over whether the world map behind the anchorman was a map or a depiction of clouds. On the other hand, when shown a map or aerial image of countryside they know, the nomads accurately orient and interpret it, naming the mountains and drainages depicted. Saalih especially enjoyed my star chart. He would tell me what time the Pleiades would rise, for example, and ask me what time the chart indicated. The two were almost always in agreement.

Many desert travelers have been astonished by the nomad's navigational and tracking ability, calling it a "sixth sense." The Khushmaan are exceptional way-finders and topographical interpreters able, for instance, to tell from tracks whether a camel was carrying baggage or a man; whether gazelle tracks were made by a male or female; which way a car was traveling and what make it was; which man left a set of footprints, even if he wore sandals; and how old the tracks are. Bedouins are proud of their geographical skills which, they believe, distinguish them from settled people. If an Egyptian were at the foot of a mountain looking out over the sea, one man said, he would not know which was higher: his location or the sea. Musallim Sulimaan said that Egyptians need streets and lights to be able to orient and move, adding, "To us, wadi are streets: we read them." Saalih told me, "Your people don't need to know the country but we do, to know exactly where things are in order to live." Pointing to his head, he said, "My map is here."

The difference in the way-finding abilities of nomads and settled persons may be due to the greater survival value of these skills for nomads and to the more complex meanings they attribute to locations. Bedouin places are rich in ideological and practical significance. The nomads interpret and interact with these meanings on a regular basis and create new places in their lifetimes. Theirs is an experience of belonging and becoming with the landscape, whereas settled people are more likely to inherit and accommodate themselves to a set of given places.

The nomads' homeland is so vast, and the margin of survivability in it so narrow, that topographic knowledge must be encyclopedic. Places either *are* the resources that allow human life in the desert, or are the signposts that lead to resources. A Khushmaan man pinpointed the role of places in desert survival: "Places have names so that people do not get lost. They can learn where water and other things are by using place names." Tragedy may result if the nomad has insufficient or incorrect information about places: many deaths by thirst are attributed to faulty directions for finding water.

What places are named, the ways in which they have acquired names, and the information these names contain reveal a great deal about the nomads' identification with their landscape. Before the Maʿaza began arriving about two hundred years ago, the area had non-Arabic, ʿAbabda place names. The Maʿaza retained a few of these, but essentially had a tabula rasa on which to record their topographic autobiography. This "text" is made up of the names themselves and also the unwritten explanations of events that occurred at these places, passed down in folklore through several generations. These names and spoken footnotes describe physical environment, subsistence activities, political history, social experiences, and world views.

There are more names for watercourses than any other topographical features. The Maʿaza have a vast vocabulary for drainages, based on aspect, slope, length, altitude, and soils; the outsider familiar only with the word "wadi" has tens of new terms to learn. There is almost as impressive an offering of designations for elevations, from sizes of boulders to jebels and compositions from limestone to granite. Maʿaza toponomy is largely wadi-centric, with mountain blocks, for example, named after the watercourses draining them, rather than the reverse. This fact reflects the nomads' subsistence pattern: their lives are focused on drainages, where pasture for their animals is largely confined. The third largest group of place-objects is water sources. How far one must dig or climb for water and whether it occurs in igneous, metamorphic, or sedimentary country are among the many qualifications defining a given type of water source. A fourth substantial category of objects named as places is an unusual one: woody trees, such as acacias and ben-trees. The importance of these "living landmarks" is discussed in detail later.

Many places are named for the vegetation that sustains the pastoral livelihood, and the most common Khushmaan place is a drainage named after a type of plant. Wadis named for perennial trees and shrubs such as acacias, tamarisks, and capers are far more numerous than those called after ephemeral plants, probably because the former represent more lasting landmarks.

Names of places relate the ecologies of wild and domestic animals on the Maʿaza landscape. Jebel adh-Dhibaah ("Slaughter Mountain") is so-named because when the nomads' goats pasture there they die from the mysterious ailment described earlier. Jebel Maʿsiya ("Mountain of Recalcitrance") takes its name from the defiant ibex that escape hunters by fleeing there.

Place names also reflect the nomads' perceptions of physical environment. Graygar, the plain at the head of Wadi Fatiira, means "cold": brisk winds often sweep down from the surrounding mountains across its expanse. Jebel al-ʿUmaan ("Mountain of Delusion") is called this because its water source is so difficult to reach that almost everyone who tries is disappointed.

The social and political histories of the Maʿaza are recorded in place names. The earliest political place on the Maʿaza landscape is probably in Wadi al-Ghuzaa at Magbar Ruwayshid, the tomb of the early Maʿaza raiding leader Ruwayshid, who was killed by ʿAbabda foe. Many places refer to the conflict between the Maʿaza and the English during the salt monopoly. "The Shade of the Policeman" (Tuur al-Askar), for example, takes its name from the guards who rested there while enforcing Thomas Russell's order to prevent Bedouins from hunting ibex. "There's the Shade of the Policeman: let's stay away from there," the nomads would say; this was Saalih's idea of how the place earned its name.

Rather than randomly name a place after a person not necessarily affiliated with it, as sedentary folk often do, the nomads name a place by commemorating a particular person who had some experience there. Khushmaan topographic identity is comprised not so much of spatial markers of experiences common to all clanspeople as of particular events that affected individuals. These individuals' encounters build a collective sense of belonging on the landscape. Every Khushmaan individual knows where he or she was born, wed, became a parent, lost a mother or father, or spent a memorable time. A man often refers to the place he was born or has some other positive affinity with as "my wadi" or "my jebel." "I was born south of Jebel Ghaarib at Jebel Irsays," Saalih said. "My son Sulimaan was born at Wadi Ghuwayrib, his mother at Jebel Daara, and my father at Wadi ad-Dibb. This area is our kingdom." Near Galt Tuuriya he reminisced: "I was here as a boy in the spring of 1957 for four months with my family and six others and our sheep, goats, and camels. Our wool houses were here. Look at the rock outlines where they stood. I built a stone-lined path here, about a meter wide and twenty long, leading to the Tuuriya water, so that no one would hurt their feet walking there after dark. My father was here. There had been a flash flood. Every two months we went to Hurghada for supplies."

Meanings of personal places endure thanks to the nomads' exacting oral traditions. Umm Tahuur Salaama ("Circumcision-place of Salaama") was named for the circumcision of the Khushaymi Salaama 'Iyd, who died about 1960 at the age of ninety; the event would have occurred about 1880. The rock of Aruus 'Ayd ("bride of 'Ayd") is even older: no one is certain to which tribe 'Ayd belonged. My companions explained that 'Ayd had stayed at the rock for a couple of months. He was a bachelor at an age when he should have been married, but in staying at this lonely place he was clearly not in a hurry to wed. Because of the man's intimacy with the place, it was dubbed his "bride."

In 1986 Saalih and I revisited Wadi Shatuun after a three-year absence. There had been no rain, and our tracks were still in the sand. Saalih pointed to them and said, "When we made these my father was alive, and so was yours." In saying this, Saalih not only revealed his bond with that place but also gave me an affection for the spot.

Typically of the nomads, Saalih was also associating the place with a particular time. To the Khushmaan, the landscape is a "vast mnemonic system."[1] Unlike sedentary people, the nomads routinely think in terms of where they were when something happened or when they heard about an event, in addition to what happened and to whom. An example is the assassination of President Kennedy. Americans old enough to remember do remember where they were when they heard the news. So do the Khushmaan, who in many cases learned of the event weeks later. The difference is that Americans remember their locations because the event was extraordinary, while the Arabs remember this association along with numerous other events that year which we would perceive as mundane.

To understand how nomads use their environment, it is necessary to consider the peculiar, and to settled people unfamiliar, way they attribute identical meanings to places and natural phenomena, and to places and periods of time. For example, *al-mahal* means both an area made barren by drought and the actual vegetation desiccated by drought. *Ar-rabiˀa* means both a locale where rich ephemeral pasture is growing and the spring season when this pasture occurs. Traveling with Basseri nomads in southern Iran, the anthropologist Fredrik Barth noted a similar phenomenon: "When I asked them whether truffles appear only briefly in the beginning of April, or perhaps are found only in the Sarvestan valley, the only answer I could obtain was 'yes.' My two alternatives were to them merely two ways of expressing the same experience: a season is a stretch of country, and *vice versa*" (Barth 1961, 149).

In Khushmaan vocabulary and reasoning, locations and perennial trees are very often synonymous. Many single, isolated acacias and other trees *are* places: Yasarit al-ʿAbd ("The Ben-tree of the Slave"), Yasarit Umm ʿAruug ("The Ben-tree Having Roots"), Sayaalat Umm Garadhiyaat ("The Acacia of Wadi Umm Garadhiyaat"), and Sayaalat Ruwaʿiy ("The Acacia Tree of Ruwaʿiy"), for example. If you asked whether Sayaalat Ruwaʿiy is a tree or a place, the answer might well be yes. Ruwaʿiy's Acacia has another dimension: it is also a personal place commemorating a man who spent much time at the tree. In subsequent discussion, it will be seen that the associations of personality, place, and tree in such "living landmarks" influence Khushmaan uses of natural resources.

Nomads are not the hurried, rootless wanderers many believe them to be. Contrary even to their own group ideology, which insists that places within clan territory belong equally to all clanspeople, individuals frequent some locales longer or more often than others and become associated with these places by their kin. Having the choice of moving to equally good pasture at Jebel Abul Hassan and other areas, Muhammad Umbaarak, for instance, always moved his family and livestock to Abul Hassan. Subhi ʿAwaad's household gravitates toward Jebel Gattaar. These attachments are often inherited: Subhi, for example, acquired his preference for the Gattaar region from his father, ʿAwaad Saliim, who had frequented the massif for decades. Sulimaan Maraʿi and his sons passed much of their lives in the mountainous district of Abu Dukhaan, and ʿAli Musallim likewise near Wadi ar-Radda. Muhammad Saalim has spent more than fifty years in the Graygar and Wadi al-Ghuzaa area; his peers say that "that is his kingdom." When a man dies, his sons typically bury him there in what is or becomes a family plot, and they commemorate him in part by continuing to frequent his place. This is the process by which a small area becomes, in the course of two or more generations, the symbolic and behavioral realm of the family line or lineage.

Such "lineage territories" are not distributed randomly. The nomads endear themselves especially to those places containing perennial drought-enduring resources, especially woody trees. Typically, the favored place is part of a single wadi or mountain where many acacias grow. In the lineage territory, the individual, family, and lineage accept responsibilities for these perennial resources and monitor others' uses of them, even though their ideology of common clan ownership of space and natural resources does not allow such powers. The ways in which the nomads pledge and effect these responsibilities, and the role that "lineage preserves" play in Maʿaza resource management, are discussed in a subsequent chapter.

Biases reflecting the authors' settled lives are apparent in literature about nomads' relations with space. An anthropologist insisted that the nomad "does not identify himself with a particular small piece of territory" and suggested that this sense of rootlessness causes nomads to abuse their environment (Spooner 1973, 37). Khushmaan perceptions of space suggest the contrary: they are deeply attached to particular places, and this rootedness promotes a sense of responsibility for their environment. Although nomads' places are not laid out on grids or marked on maps but exist only in oral tradition, they may be more vital and enduring than the taken-for-granted locations of settled life. Bedouins have no sense of placelessness: their desert is an only home, a landscape of genesis, involvement, and meaning.

6. *A Bedouin Natural History*

Nomadic peoples are often thought to view nature in an antagonistic way, placing a premium on self-preservation in a hostile environment and disregarding local plants and animals. The Khushmaan, however, do not have the notion of man against nature but see themselves as members of the natural world. They regard man, the "Sons of Adam" (*Bani Aadam*), as a type of swine; his peers are unclean, nonruminating animals including pigs, donkeys, monkeys, carnivores, and rodents. God did not bestow great physical power upon man but did give him a soul and superior intellect. The Khushmaan believe that He also gave man the burden of learning how to live responsibly with other living things.

Despite their principle of compatibility with the environment, the Khushmaan, like people everywhere, have sometimes abused their natural resources. Around them is evidence of long-term changes from rich pastures to poor, and from abundant wildlife to few animals. Unlike most people these nomads cannot distribute the blame for recent environmental wrongdoing among others, but have accepted and reappraised their responsibilities.

The Animal Kingdom

The Bedouins' system of classifying animals differs significantly from its Western counterpart. The nomads recognize six major animal categories: swine, true animals, flying creatures, crawling creatures, swimming creatures, and an anomalous group consisting of the hyrax and dabb-lizard (see Appendix 1).

Within the swine (*khanziir*) category, the Khushmaan define the following groups: Man (*Bani Aadam*); humanlike swine, comprised of the *nam-nam* (chimpanzee) and *sil'awi* (gorilla) which feed upon man but have religion and other cultural practices; and swine (*khanziir*) proper, which includes the monkeys (*gird*), domestic pig (*khanziir*), donkey (*himaar*), horse (*husaan*), and all carnivores (*kilaab*).

The Khushmaan lack an evolutionary perspective on human physical development; for example, they do not put man in a category of primates or regard modern man as different physically from any predecessors. However, they do believe that people formerly lived in a wild state very distinct from the civilized outdoor life Bedouins lead today: "Early people were like animals, before the Koran, Bible, and Torah. Maybe in the Sudan or Tanzania there are still people like animals. A Kuwaiti man told me there are people in the Sudan who live without clothes in the forest: those are the wild people, living like animals."

The Khushmaan regard man as the foulest of all creatures. No animal has more putrid feces; it is so bad that only the Egyptian vulture and other swine—the donkey and dog—will eat it. Ibex and other animals can detect man's horrible scent from a great distance; the ibex has a kind of allergy to it, snorting to expel the stench and then fleeing. The Arabs say that gazelles never approach an acacia that has people's belongings hanging from it. The intelligent raven, one man observed, will perch comfortably on a camel's back "but like all animals is afraid of the Sons of Adam."

The Khushmaan believe that animals fear humans because of their formidable intellectual power, despite their diminutive stature. Using wit and a throwing-stone, a man can stalk and dispatch a gazelle on the open plain where that animal could outrun him easily. In brain against brawn, a man can trap the hyena, far more powerful than he, which threatens his sheep. Saalih observed, "*Bani Aadam* is fetid and dangerous. There is none more dangerous than he. He is the king of death."

Carnivores (*kilaab*), literally meaning "dogs" but including domestic cats and dogs as well as seven local wild species of canines, felines, and hyenas, are almost as foul and intimidating as people are. Although the *salaaga* dog is virtually indispensable in the ibex hunt and the *rumaanti* (apparently after the loan-word "romantic," i.e., nonutilitarian) breed is a vigilant camp guardian, the dog is not "man's best friend." Bedouins never stroke a dog or allow it to lick them and always keep it at a distance. *Kilaab* also include locally well-known animals such as the fox, hyena, and caracal; those such as the leopard known to inhabit neighboring lands; and a beast called the *shiib* which should interest cryptozoologists, biogeographers, and mammalogists.[1]

Intermediate between "swine" and "true animals" is a category of nonhuman creatures with humanlike moral attributes, the rock hyrax (*wabr, Procavia capensis*) and dabb-lizard (*dhabb, Uromastyx aegyptius* and *U. ocellatus*). Their position in the Arabs' classification scheme is anomalous: they are "like *Bani Aadam,* but not *Bani Aadam;* not swine [*khanziir*], but true animals [*hayawaanaat*]." The dens and burrows of hyraxes and dabb-lizards are the only animal residences the Bedouins call "homes" (*bayt*), a term which connotes human social organization, rather than "holes," as they call most other animals' refuges.

Of all their nondomesticated animals, the Khushmaan most revere the rock hyrax. It is the most "like *Bani Aadam*." Like man, the hyrax has no tail. Hyraxes post a guard outside their colony, and when danger approaches, this sentinel, taking a humanlike risk of self-sacrifice, calls loudly to warn the others. Like the nomads they are especially fond of the sound of a lute (*rabaaba*), but also are drawn to the sound of a radio; to attract them, simply turn up the volume, and they will come to investigate. In one very significant respect, however, the hyrax is not like man: it chews cud.

For these qualities the hyrax is sacrosanct. "Oh, eater of the hyrax, oh, eater of your dear brother," is a solemn Khushmaan saying. Shocked to learn that Subhi ʿAwaad had slain and eaten a hyrax, graybeard Sulimaan Maraʿi said this repeatedly, adding "Eating the hyrax is the most forbidden thing!"

Of the dabb-lizard, Sulimaan Maraʿi said, "The *dhabb* is like a man. It has five fingers on the hand, like *Bani Aadam*." The Arabs disagree about whether the animal ruminates, but concur that it has many uncanny, humanlike qualities. Umtayr Muhammad developed a special respect for this creature:

> Some Khushmaan have eaten *dhabb*, but this is forbidden [*haraam*]. It is much respected for saving the Prophet's life. Once, the Prophet was fleeing from a man who wanted to kill him. The Prophet entered a cave, and a *dhabb* emerged and with his tail erased the Prophet's tracks in the sand. . . . I once threw a rock at a *dhabb*, hitting it in the head. The *dhabb* put its hands to its head, like a man with a headache. He looked like a man. After that, I did not molest any *dhabb*. When the *dhabb* is dead and the body or flesh is placed in a fire, it twitches and shakes.

Sulimaan Maraʿi agreed that the lizard still behaved as if it were alive up to three days after its death and concluded, "It is not good to eat the *dhabb*."

The category of "true animals" (*hayawaanaat*) includes the hare, sheep, goat, camel, gazelle, ibex, and Barbary sheep. While they recognize no physical and moral affinities with them, the Arabs are particularly fond of these animals. In contrast to their disdain for dogs, children and adults alike fawn over a sheep, goat, camel, or captive infant ibex or gazelle, holding and kissing these animals, especially on the lips. Ibex and gazelles are the nomads' only wild pets.

Once, as we ate ibex brain, I asked Saalih whether the animal's brain were "clean." My meaning was whether it had a keen mind, but he answered quickly: "The entire animal is clean. He eats only plants." Vegetarian diet and rumination thus distinguish clean creatures from foul, carnivorous nonruminants. The nomads eat all but the hide, bone, and stomach contents of the ibex and gazelle. They say that even the dung of ruminants is clean and use it as cooking fuel when no firewood is available.

The Khushmaan have no confident explanations for the age or origin of domestic animals, or for the affinities of livestock with wild animals. One man proposed that "people always had domestic animals." Many Khushmaan regard wild herbivores as domestic stock that got away from man, rather than domestic animals as descendants of tamed wild stock. The similarities between domestic goat and ibex are well known, but no one can explain the differences: "Our wild animals are always monotoned, like the countryside: sandgrouse, sand partridge, ibex, gazelle, hare, fox, and caracal. But domestic animals are usually black and white, and often striped: rabbit, sheep, goat, pigeon, chicken, and dog. Why?"

The category of "flying creatures" (*tuyuur*) encompasses all birds and flying animals, including bats and winged insects. "Swimming creatures" (*samak,* lit. "fish") include an endemic desert fairy shrimp and all known sea creatures, including turtles. "Crawling creatures" (*duud,* lit. "worms") include reptiles, molluscs, and wingless arthropods and chordates. *Duud* include the most despised animals of the Khushmaan homeland, bothersome and sometimes fatal vermin such as vipers, scorpions, and ants. The most feared and hated by far are the greater cerastes viper (*hanash, Cerastes cerastes*) and Burton's carpet viper (*hidhif, Echis coloratus*). Khushmaan epithets for these dangerous animals include "prick" and "land mine." The latter is especially fitting, as by day the inactive reptile lies curled just below the surface of the sand and can be detected only by the always-wary eyes of the Bedouins. Vipers are the only animals the nomads kill at every opportunity. Once, as Saalih was beating a viper to death, he cursed, "You son of a dog! Why must you kill *Bani Aadam,* ibex, and gazelles?"

Taxonomy and Taboos

Some categories of the Khushmaan animal classification system consist of animals which may or may not be eaten, according to the Bedouins' folk versions of Islamic beliefs. Eating any "swine," including all carnivores, is prohibited. All "true animals" may be eaten only if slaughtered ritually: the living animal's throat must be cut while the words "In the name of God, the Compassionate, the Merciful" are spoken. The guidelines for eating flying, swimming, and crawling creatures are less categorical and seem to the nomads to stray from the essential ruminating/nonruminating dichotomy in their classification scheme. The Khushmaan, however, take the individual prescriptions for granted, and when asked to explain the reasoning behind them sometimes cannot: "But the flying creature does not have cud, yet you can eat it. And the swimming creature has no cud, yet it is permissible. Even without being slaughtered! Even if it is dead, you can cook and eat it, and that is all right. I don't know why."

Nor could people explain why they may eat some flying creatures but not others. In the past, they said, they ate locusts and grasshoppers and did not have to kill them ritually. Eating bats and some other flying creatures is taboo. They sometimes slaughter and eat quail (*firra, Coturnix coturnix*), sand partridge (*hajal, Ammoperdix heyi*), houbara bustard (*hubaaraa, Chlamydotis undulata*), and spotted and coronetted sandgrouse (*gataa, Pterocles senegallus* and *P. coronatus*). These birds are herbivorous, but as the nomads noted this is not characteristic of all permissible birds. In exceptional cases people have eaten the flesh of the omnivorous white stork (*raahu, Ciconia ciconia*) and grey crane (*wizz ʿiraag, Grus grus*), although aware that the white stork will eat even a dead dog. The Khushmaan insist that there are no explicit laws against eating ravens, raptorial birds, and owls, yet they eat none of these. They also deny any religious reason for not eating crawling creatures.

Explanations for these food avoidances may be found in Islamic beliefs that have come down to the Khushmaan not as religious laws but as taken-for-granted rules for everyday behavior. The nomads are apparently unaware that many regulations were established by God and his Prophet to be observed by all Muslims. Islamic law exempts all sea creatures from the prohibited category of dead animals not slaughtered ritually: speaking of the sea, the Prophet Muhammad said, "Its water is pure and its dead are permissible" (Al-Qaradawi 1985, 48). Locusts are also exempted, and the question of slaughtering them does not arise in Islamic law: "We went with the Prophet on seven expeditions, and we ate locusts with him," wrote Ibn Abu Awfa (Al-Qaradawi 1985, 48). Avoidance of ravens, raptors, and owls may also be attributed to Islamic law; the Prophet "forbade the eating of any wild animals with a canine tooth and of any bird with talons" (Al-Qaradawi 1985, 53).

The Bedouins believe it is wrong to kill any animal without good reason. They regard this as a social and moral imperative, not a religious one. This conviction may however derive from, and is certainly duplicated in, Islamic law; the Prophet said: "Whoever kills a sparrow or anything bigger than that without a just cause, Allah will hold him accountable on the Day of Judgement. The listeners asked, O Messenger of Allah, what is a just cause? He replied, That he kill it to eat, not to simply chop off its head and then throw it away" (Al-Qaradawi 1985, 65).

Independent of taxonomy and taboos, animals and plants have other meanings for the nomads. The Bedouin is not reluctant to anthropomorphize living things and assumes that the "human" qualities recognized in them are their own. "All animals are good, I think," one man said. The wheatear (*slaygaw*) is a good bird; one reason is its habit of fluttering over any viper it sees and calling loudly, thus warning people of danger. The brown-necked raven (*ghuraab, Corvus ruficollis*) invites envy. Little owls (*buuma, Athene noctua*) and eagle owls (*hid-hid, Bubo bubo*) associate with demons (*afariit*). The most mischievous animals, claimed Suwaylim ʿAwaad, are the raven, fox, and mouse. The fox (*abul husayn, Vulpes rueppelli*) is also the smartest; Saalih explained why there were no fox remains among those of numerous other animals that had stumbled into and died in a cave in the South Galala Plateau: "The fox has a brain just like that of *Bani Aadam.*"

Many acacias and other trees are not simply trees. Some are associated with particular people, families, and lineages. Others, notably the four crown-of-thorns trees (*sidr, Zizyphus spina-Christi*) in Khushmaan territory, are regarded as "antiquities" which were cultivated by the Romans. Sulimaan ʿAwaad explained another reason for the particular importance of this tree: the moon's surface suggests a *sidr* tree, with the darkest portions resembling the tree's roots, trunk, and branches. Some Bedouins recognize spiritual qualities in plants. Sulimaan Maraʿi, for example, regards the clump of toothbrush trees (*araak, Salvadora persica*) where Wadi Haamid meets the Wadi Qena plain as the abode of a type of spirit called "lord of the place" (*saahib al-mahal*).

George Murray, whose constant ʿAbabda companions probably cast their traditional enemies in a poor light for the Scotsman, believed the Maʿaza were too crude to appreciate the beauty of their land. The sight of a rare snow on the Red Sea mountains was, he wrote, "wasted on the Maʿaza Arabs and the ibex. Yet the Maʿaza, though rogues and vagabonds, are not quite without poetry and I have heard among them a rude rhyme" (Murray 1967, 106). This perception is in marked contrast to a remark by the Khushaymi ʿAwaad Saliim to Leo Tregenza, which clearly impressed the Englishman for its sensitivity: "I like to feel the stars turning over me, especially when the dew falls, ever so softly; making your garments soft, soft" (1955, 165).

Despite the hardships their environment poses, the Khushmaan are awed and inspired by it. They seem to have as much an eye for natural wonder and beauty as any culture that produces art and poetry. Of many examples I could offer, two will suffice. When Saalih and I reached the only specimen of the *sarh* tree (*Maerua crassifolia*) known in the Maʿaza desert, he was boyishly enthusiastic about our strange find: "Even if a man wanted to plant this tree here, how could he? Look where it's growing: in solid bare rock! Where's the soil? This tree must be like an oil drill! How did it get here? There are no others. Look, its wood has the color of tamarisk but is stronger than the ben-tree." The other occasion was a spring day when one of my companions remarked as we passed the flowering ben-trees of Wadi Bali, "They are beautiful: I wish they were always that way."

Ecological Knowledge

The nomads' knowledge and uses of resources are not based only on taxonomic categories or aesthetic qualities. These people are also unmatched authorities about the ecology of their environment. Two examples will illustrate the breadth and depth of their knowledge: a single impromptu commentary about animal diet and a series of observations about the ibex.

The breadth of Khushmaan natural history is well illustrated by an extemporaneous answer to a question I posed about what animals eat:

> The Egyptian vulture eats human feces. The white stork eats *arabuuna* lizards, *'ayr al-banaat* beetles, and the moth larvae which feed upon *silli* and *rabl* plants. Sand partridges eat the seeds of *hurbith* and *silli*. Sandgrouse eat seeds of *hurbith*, *gutbi gamh*, *gutbi faga'aa*, and *faynii*. Brown-necked ravens won't eat human feces but will eat camel dung if it contains grain. Donkeys eat human feces. Foxes eat gerbils, dipodils, and lesser jerboas, and the carcasses of goats and gazelles, but will not eat *'ayr al-banaat* beetles. The fox won't eat a dead dog, or vice versa. Although a dog will attack and kill a fox, he will not eat it. The camel will not eat the colocynth gourd; it's too bitter. The donkey will eat both the gourd and roots, and so will goats; sheep eat only the gourd. The ibex eat its leaves, dried and green gourds, and certainly the roots; but the gazelle eats the green gourd and roots only, not the leaves. The roots contain much water, and the gazelle thrives on them. Of all animals, only the domestic dog will eat its young.

The Khushmaan know a great deal not only about the interrelations of plants and animals but about the life-cycles, habits, habitats, and other details of particular animals and plants. The following observations about the ibex are exclusively those of the nomads. These suggest that much "scientific" knowledge is held in the untrained, "unscientific" environmental lore of these people, and they illustrate the importance of this animal to the Bedouins.

The Ibex

The nomads' generic name for the ibex is *sayd* ("game"), which indicates their principal perception of this wild goat. However, they also have at least twenty-four other names for the animal, almost as many as for the domestic goat.[2] They recognize the animal's affinities with their goats, noting, for example, that ibex and domestic goat tracks are indistinguishable, except that a very large print can indicate only an ibex. Ibex have longer life spans (15–20 years) but similar gestation periods (5–6 months). When people are not in the area, ibex will intermingle with domestic goats but not with sheep or camels.

The ibex's summer coat is tan; the winter coat, darker. Albinos are known; Muhammad Umtayr once captured a large male "as white as a sheep." Males are larger than females, and both sexes attain a larger size in the limestone regions of the northern Ma'aza territory, particularly the South Galala Plateau, than in the granites of the south.[3] Males are sized by the handspans of their horns: a five-hander in the south weighs up to sixty-six pounds (30 kg), while its counterpart in the Galala weighs twice that. The reason is the greater variety and abundance of green plants in the Galala region. The largest are the rare six-hand males.

The ibex's favorite food is lotus (*gadhub, Lotus deserti*). Small conical excavations in wadi sands indicate where the animals dug out these plants to eat the roots. The ibex is also fond of the flowers of ben-trees, the leaves and fruit of wild figs, and the leaves of acacias and capers (*lassaf, Capparis cartilaginea*), but will not eat caper fruits. It is the only animal that will eat henbane (*saykaraan, Hyoscyamus boveanus*). A man once witnessed an ibex eating the excrement of coronetted sandgrouse at a water source. Ibex descend to feed in wadi floors very early in the morning and again in the heat of day, when people are least likely to be active. To avoid man they will also feed at night in the wadis, particularly when there is bright moonlight, a time when people often hunt them successfully.

Ibex are more tolerant of the sun than gazelles, not seeking shade as readily, but have higher water requirements. They cover long distances to water, routinely traveling up to six miles (10 km) between feeding and watering locales. In the height of summer, they must drink once every three to six days. In winters of good pasture, they can go entirely without water, fulfilling their needs from water-saturated vegetation, but in winters of drought they must drink once every ten days. Ibex drink at night as well as during the day. During periods of prolonged drought, the animals become weak, and their meat is considered poor eating. Hard rains sometimes fall and form pools and short-lived rivers in which ibex are presumed to be able to swim, as goats are known to do, even though no one has ever seen an ibex do so.

About the time Canopus (*Is-hayl*) rises in September, the male ibex takes to the high mountains to "mate and get dirty." During this autumn rut season, two males face off against one another, each attended by four or five females. Females look on as their prospective mates rise repeatedly on their hind legs, charging at each other to smash heads and horns in combat. The eventual winner takes all the females, including those which had attended his rival. Sometimes both combatants lose when their horns interlock, and they die of starvation before they can extricate themselves: people have found still-engaged skeletons telling this story.

The male takes up with his five to fifteen females high in the mountains until early spring. There he eats very little, losing weight and growing increasingly filthy, urinating on himself. His once-lustrous hide grows mangy and rife with ticks and flies, and soon he is "like carrion." He becomes so weak that any dog, and sometimes a determined man alone, can catch him. At this time his meat is most inedible. During summer months males are the best eating, particularly in August, when they are fattening themselves in the wadis in preparation for the impending rut season.

Two and sometimes three young are born, almost always between April and June; this is different from the gazelle, which may give birth almost any time of year. Unlike the Barbary sheep, a mother ibex will return to look for her young if the two become separated. Once a man touches an infant ibex, however, the mother will not accept her offspring, which then circles about bleating until it dies. A kind of male infanticide sometimes occurs when the adult animals reject their male offspring and young males in the herd. The herd is comprised of a number of females and young, usually led by a large male. The largest number of animals seen together at once was thirty-five to forty, all females and young, on the South Galala Plateau. Bachelor herds of up to seven males are known.

People sometimes introduce an orphaned infant ibex into their family herd, where it takes to a single goat or sheep "wet-nurse." Typically, the adopted ibex does not grow to adulthood within the foster herd but seeks independence. Adopted gazelles, in contrast, often mature within the herd. The orphaned ibex, unlike its gazelle counterpart, develops a deep attachment to a particular person, usually the woman who looks after it and ensures that it is fed regularly. Another peaceful contact between people and ibex occurs when a man is downwind from the animals and communicates with them by imitating their whistle or bleat, or by clapping his hands to replicate their hoof beats on rocks. Unable to catch the man's scent or identify him by sight, the wild goats often hold their ground and watch curiously, giving people a rare chance to watch them.

The ibex's natural enemies include jackals, which occasionally venture forth from the margins of the Nile Valley to feed on these wild goats, as they did in Wadi Shatuun in 1986. Caracals (*gutt, Felis caracal*) are known predators throughout Maʿaza territory. One of these cats attacked an ibex in Wadi Umm Ruutha, in the South Galala Plateau, eating only its heart and viscera. At Jebel adh-Dhibaah, just south of the Maʿaza boundary, Sulimaan Suwaylim once saw an ibex swerve and fall, then noticed that to its belly was attached a caracal which had grasped its victim by the throat and had sprawled its legs between those of the ibex to prevent it from running. The Arabs presume that in earlier times, when leopards roamed the land, they too preyed upon ibex.

Today man is the ibex's main enemy. The wary animals sometimes fall victim to land mines, but hunting is a greater threat. The ibex's principal protection is its remarkable climbing ability. A secondary defense is cryptic coloration, combined with "playing possum." Muhammad Umbaarak once loosed his dog after three males. The one which was farthest behind and most likely to be taken suddenly dropped to the ground and kept perfectly still "like a rock" while the dog rushed by in pursuit of the others. Saalih once chased two ibex a long distance, losing them over the brow of a hill. As he walked, scanning the horizon, he nearly stepped on the adult female he had been pursuing: "At my feet, she was the color of the ground, with her head down. She leapt up and sped off. If I had seen her I could have taken her."

People regard ibex as among the most wary and intelligent of all animals. The ibex can run up to twenty-five miles per hour (40 KPH) on flat ground, but only for a short distance, after which it is almost unable to move. Most often the animal does not put itself in such a position, but remains close to cliffs. When pursued by man the ibex cuts right angles and seeks higher ground as evasive action. Knowing how and where to avoid man, the ibex flourishes in those places most remote from human activities: "There is no place an ibex won't go. Whether it's steep or flat, whether there is water or not, vegetation or none, the ibex must go there," a Bedouin said. Where people have slaughtered an ibex, sheep, or goat, no ibex will approach the place for at least one week. In case their lingering scent is insufficient to deter ibex, people sometimes erect wooden "scarecrows" around surface-water sources to prevent the animals from muddying or burying a precious water supply.

Ibex are accident prone, especially males, because of their great horns. Many fatalities occur in summer when the animals slip down steep, slick walls of rock basins from which they are trying to drink. One water source is called "Ibex Gripper" (Masaka Baduun) because of frequent incidents there. At a similar spot on Jebel Mi'tig, 'Iyd Sulimaan took pity on the animals and broke up the natural slide so that no more would die. Ibex also succumb to starvation and dehydration in acacia, fig, and ben-trees after their hooves or horns get caught in branches on which they are feeding. People are merciful if they reach the animals in time. At al-Hayta, Saalih Sulimaan and 'Awda Sulimaan freed an ibex trapped by its horns in an acacia, gave it food and water, and released it. That was more than fifty years ago. People still marvel that at dusk the animal returned to the men, who gave it more water.

Ibex are pestered by flies (especially *shadhabba, Hippobosca purpiparcus*) and ticks, but their principal nuisance is the botfly (*adhgat, Oestrus ovis*). Female botflies squirt their larvae into the mouths and nostrils of ibex, just as they do to people. The unfortunate ibex, unlike man, cannot expel the maggots, which crawl up the sinuses and lodge themselves in horn cores where they reside for up to a month. The ibex is often seen and heard snorting in an eventually successful attempt to expel its unwanted guests.

There are substantial numbers of ibex in Maʿaza territory. It is difficult to estimate their populations, as the animals migrate to water and pasture and their habits keep them out of sight. The nomads estimate that between two hundred and three hundred animals inhabit the Gattaar massif and that perhaps half that number live on Jebel Shaayib, which some call the "kingdom of the ibex." Several men estimated that "at least one thousand" ibex live on the South Galala Plateau. Other substantial populations, they said, are in the environs of Bir Shatuun and Jebel Daara.[4]

Environmental Changes

The nomads' views of nature and of man's relationship with the natural world are shaped in part by recent dramatic changes in the environment and by the nomads' image of what the environment should be like. That ideal habitat is based on the Arabs' perception of what the Eastern Desert was like long ago, before people began misusing their resources.

There is some reliable information about this "primordial" Eastern Desert ecosystem. The Bedouins believe, and scientists agree, that isolated living specimens and groves of such trees as the wild olive (*Olea africana*), white saksaul (*Haloxylon persicum*), white acacia (*Acacia albida*), East Indian mastiche (*Pistacia khinjuk*), and *Maerua crassifolia* are relics of once-abundant and widespread woodlands.[5] A picture of what the environment was like from the period 7000–3000 B.C. may be reconstructed from animal remains I found in a cave in the South Galala Plateau.[6] These well-preserved animals represent a far richer flora and fauna than exist in the region today. Leopards, now unknown north of the Egypt-Sudan border and sparsely distributed in the Negev of extreme southwest Asia, were abundant; at least twenty individuals died in the cave. Genets (*Genetta genetta*) and shrews (*Crocidura floweri*), small mammals which live in riverine habitats and well-watered and wooded semidesert areas, fell into the cave. These remains suggest that the prehistoric Galala, and probably much of the Eastern Desert, was formerly a savanna woodland similar to the habitat of north-central Kenya today. George Murray proposed that about 4000 B.C. the climate and vegetation of the northern Eastern Desert resembled those of present-day Palestine (Murray 1949, 22).

With their characteristic eye for detail, the Khushmaan point to numerous indications that their land is a meager relic of a bountiful past. Saalih said that fossil hillocks in Wadi Qena formed by wind-borne deposits around tamarisk trees (*athl, Tamarix aphylla*) prove that there was more rainfall in the past. This barren landscape was once forested, he explained, and the mounds remain where trees once stood. On gravel flats above Raydhaan al-Abkaar ("Rivulets of the Young Camels"), he guided me through a complex of circular ostrich "beds," apparently nests or sleeping places. These flightless birds could have lived here only in rainier times, perhaps until two hundred years ago, he surmised. Throughout Maʿaza territory are great loaf-shaped rock structures the nomads call "subjugator of the jackal" (*nusrit adh-dhiib*) which are, they suppose, ancient traps for predatory beasts: leopard, hyena, and *shiib*. The Bedouins point to networks of trails on slopes which animals no longer walk, saying that multitudes of Barbary sheep, ibex, and gazelle followed these trails in ancient times:

> When the Romans were here, there were many more trees. Everywhere they dug for water, they found it. Look at the amount of charcoal that comes from their blacksmiths' shops! To see how much rain there was, just look at how broken-up by torrents the Roman roads crossing wadi beds are. These days there are no rains that would do this. Because there was so much water and pasture, the Romans had a lot of meat: ibex, gazelle, sheep, goat, and cow. There were so many trees, you could not see the ground: *sayaal* [*Acacia raddiana*], *salam* [*Acacia ehrenbergiana*], *tundhub* [*Capparis decidua*], and *markh* [*Leptadenia pyrotechnica*]. Now, there are almost none! Have you seen Umm Yasaar? High in the drainage, the *sayaal* and *tundhub* are still present, showing the land as it should be.

Perennial vegetation in the Eastern Desert probably was more abundant and widespread two thousand years ago than it is today. However, it is unlikely that rainfall was much higher or that annual plants grew more reliably. An observation by Theophrastus (372–287 B.C.) might well be made by a modern traveler in the region: "A little north of Koptos there grows on the land no tree except that called the thirsty Acacia, and even this is scarce by reason of the heat and the lack of water, for it never rains except at intervals of four or five years, and then the rain comes down heavily and is soon over" (quoted in Jackson 1957, 57). Pliny the Elder (ca. A.D. 50) corroborated this observation: "But, in the East, it is a remarkable fact that, as soon as we leave Qift, passing through the desert, we find nothing growing except the thorn called 'dry thorn'" (Murray 1967, 19).

Paleoclimatologists suggest that Egypt has been virtually as dry as it is today since about 2400 B.C., when regular rainfall ended as a consequence of global climatic changes in the wake of the last ice age.[7] Blame for degradation of the desert environment over the past four thousand years thus falls upon man rather than nature.

The Khushmaan believe that human wrongdoing in the environment began with the "Romans," that is, ancient people. They point especially to the destruction of acacias. Saalih guided me over a barren gravel terrace above the watercourse of Umm Yasaar, near Jebel Gattaar. Neolithic flints lay there in abundance. The "Roman" people who made them lived there, he explained, when the terrace was thick with acacias. Saalih showed me evidence that they had exploited this natural wealth, turning groves into charcoal. Scraping away surface gravel, he exposed a layer of charcoal dust. To measure the acacia's former coverage, he pointed to light and dark granite boulders. The lighter ones had been in the shade of acacia trees, he said, while the darker ones had been exposed longer to direct sunlight. Now the sun baked both.

The nomads know why ancient people charcoaled trees. At every Greek and Roman quarry and mine site, there is a blacksmith shop. There, they explain, the "Romans" burned acacia charcoal to forge and repair their tools. At gold-mining sites they burned great quantities of charcoal to separate ore from parent rock.

The Khushmaan believe that such activities had a long-term, detrimental effect on acacia populations and on numbers of animals which feed on these trees. At Jebel Abu Dukhaan (Roman: Mons Porphyrites), Saalih pointed out the former dens of rock hyraxes. Dried urine staining these ancient habitats dated to the "Roman" era, he said, and the hyraxes disappeared when the ancients cut acacia trees to fuel nearby foundries.

Ancient people have not been the only agents of environmental degradation. Khushmaan oral tradition records a better environment in the more recent past. The nomads escorted me around desolate places that were once prolific: Umm Anfii'a, Umm Sidr, Bali, Umm Yasaar, Khaliij al-Mallaaha, Athilma, al-Ghuzaa, and Umm Tinaydhab were former showcases for acacias. When he was about thirty years old, Salaama Sulimaan met an eighty-year-old 'Abadi who as a boy had seen Wadi Umm Anfii'a "full" of acacias; that would have been about 1870. Musallim Sulimaan related how splendid the stands of *Acacia raddiana* and *Leptadenia pyrotechnica* once were: "Long ago, this land was all forest, of *sayaal* and *markh*. But now there is no forest. One hundred and fifty years ago, Wadi Umm Anfii'a had so many trees that you could not see your camel: the acacia trees would hide it. But then people came, and cut, and charcoaled."

Early European explorers of the central Red Sea mountains described local Bedouins, very likely Khushmaan men, cutting acacias at an urgent pace. In the 1880s E. A. Floyer traveled through Wadi Gattaar: "It was thickly studded with big mimosa-trees, some 20 and 30 feet high, but all hacked and chopped about. It seemed piteous. . . . The Bedawin occupation, and the only one I know them to engage in, is making charcoal" (1887, 670). Other observers noted that post–World War I inflation, with fuel and food shortages in the Nile Valley, encouraged Eastern Desert Bedouins to charcoal trees and hunt ibex at an accelerated rate (Russell 1949, 77).

By Khushmaan reckoning, 1910–40 was their heyday of tree cutting. As late as the 1950s, they charcoaled acacias in Wadi Guurdhi and other major tributaries of Wadi Qena and in Wadi Qena itself. Profit was only one motivation for the Bedouins to abuse these resources. The relative abundance of acacias and other trees, and people's confidence that there would be plenty left after they took just a few more, certainly played a role. Prior to the 1950s, there was no censure against cutting and charcoaling live acacias and other trees: "In those days no one would ask, 'Why are you charcoaling?' Acacias were plentiful, there was little money around, and the demand for charcoal was great."

Drought was another stimulus for people to overexploit perennial vegetation and game animals. Under the pressure of prolonged drought, the nomads' only alternative to working for wages or settling outside the desert is to use their drought-enduring resources of perennial flora and game. There is a strong temptation to overuse. The nomads look back on acacia cutting in the 1950s as an act of drought-induced despair. They had hacked off live branches to feed leaves to their camels, sheep, and goats. The effect of this activity and of charcoaling was a sharp depopulation of perennial flora, with an all-time low between 1950 and 1960. During the drought of the 1950s, Saalih related, the Arabs harvested ben-seeds with unprecedented thoroughness. Those men profited, but their activities reduced substantially the numbers of ben-trees that might have been growing in the wadis today. Other plants were affected by people's reactions to the 1950s drought: "Because of the drought, there was a problem with wormwood. It could not make enough seeds to perpetuate itself because too many men came and cut it too soon, before its seeds could develop. Then because of the drought, there were no new plants. It was the same problem with argel. An entire year is needed for its seeds to develop. Too many people would not let it grow long enough. Long ago there was much more wormwood and argel than there is today."

The Khushmaan also overhunted game. An irrecoverable victim was the Barbary sheep (*Ammotragus lervia*), which became extinct in the northern Eastern Desert about 1955. The nomads accept blame and feel remorse for its demise. Muhammad Umbaarak lamented the animal's passing: "I never saw *kabsh al-khala'a* alive, but I saw the skin of one my brother and father had just killed at ash-Shifawiyya, in the Labyrinth. I was a little younger than my boy Saalim at the time [11 years old, ca. 1925]. 'Awaad, Sulimaan

'Awda's nephew, once killed seven with dogs. What a loss!" One Arab suggested that hunting this animal was cruel: "The Barbary sheep was not fast or clever. It was like a cow, and did not have a chance."

In some cases non-Ma'aza persons have been responsible for recent abuses of the Ma'aza environment. The 'Ababda tribe has sometimes transgressed its privileges in Khushmaan territory. The Khushmaan still relate that about 1900 an 'Abadi cut a great stand of *markh* trees (*Leptadenia pyrotechnica*) in Wadi al-Baruud to supply firewood to a nearby phosphate mining camp. Just a few years ago, some unidentified 'Ababda men cut and charcoaled acacias in the Ma'aza Wadi Umm Haadh. Formerly nomadic 'Ababda tribesmen have come recently from the Nile Valley to charcoal *Acacia ehrenbergiana* in the accessible lower reaches of Wadi Qena.

Nonnomads have done some of the worst damage, reinforcing Khushmaan disdain for these people. Since 1967 Egyptian soldiers have destroyed many acacias in the desert homeland. They have driven into Wadi al-Mallaaha, Wadi Abu Haadh, Wadi al-Hawashiyya, Wadi al-Markh, and elsewhere to cut large acacias for fuel in their camps along the Red Sea coast. Army officers have also taken a toll on animals. In 1982 a party of military men horrified members of a Khushmaan household near Wadi al-Hawashiyya when they showed off seventeen gazelles they had shot nearby. As offensive to the Arabs as the carnage itself was these presumed Muslims' failure to slaughter the animals ritually. In the following year, another group of officers killed three gazelles in Wadi al-Atrash, and two in Wadi al-Ghuzaa. A Khushaymi had agreed to guide them on the condition that they take only one animal. Ignoring his protests, they returned the following month and hunted without a guide. In 1986 a similar incident occurred when a party of hunters from Alexandria with a Khushaymi guide promised to take one gazelle but killed thirteen, including an infant animal, with rifles and crossbows.

The worst offenses, according to the Khushmaan, have been committed by hunters from the Gulf States. In April 1982 a wealthy Qatari hunter employed three Khushmaan guides to help him bag "one or two" gazelles in Wadi Qena. The trip was planned to last fifteen days, but the guides allowed only three. During that time the hunter, whose outfit included two wives, two maidservants, three drivers, four automobiles, and two rifles, killed twenty gazelles in a nineteen-mile (30 km) stretch of Wadi Qena. The hunters dazzled their prey at night with powerful spotlights and shot them with scoped rifles; one of the guides explained, "The car came to within thirty-three feet (10 m) of the animals. They didn't know where to run. When they saw their own shadows behind them, they were frightened and some ran headlong into the car." Refrigerators in the vehicles allowed the meat to be driven to Cairo and then flown to Qatar, where, the hunter had told his guides, all gazelles had been hunted out. It also outraged the nomads that one Qatari hunter shot and killed a white stork for no apparent reason, not even retrieving the body.

In Wadi ʿAraba bands of Qatari and Kuwaiti hunters have diminished populations of game animals. ʿAwaad Raadhi claimed that in 1968 the gazelles of Wadi ʿAraba were so numerous that they were "like goats." From 1980 to 1983, another man estimated, foreign hunters eliminated nearly all of that wadi's one thousand to fifteen hundred gazelles. He blamed the same hunters for decimating the once-abundant houbara bustard (*hubaaraa, Chlamydotis undulata*) in Wadi ʿAraba. In May 1983 Saalih and I failed to find any gazelle tracks in the remote upper reaches of Wadi at-Tarfa, which, he said, had five years earlier been the "kingdom of the gazelles." He attributed this local extirpation to forays by Qatari hunters.

Non-Bedouin technology has diminished numbers of gazelles on the Red Sea coastal plain where, Musallim Sulimaan reminisced, the antelopes were plentiful twenty-five years ago. Even as late as 1976, he said, the animals lingered near Dayr Abu Shaʿar (ruins of the Greek port of Myos Hormos) on the coast eight miles (13 km) north of Hurghada. However, an increase in automobile traffic along the coastal road, and the activity of soldiers stationed near it, have driven gazelles away. Musallim observed that they have sought refuge in the middle and upper portions of larger mountain wadis where they did not venture formerly and where they have overlapped increasingly with the ibex, which descend to these places to feed.

The Khushmaan are concerned about man's destructive abilities not only in their small homeland but wherever people live. They believe that droughts and other "natural" calamities are caused ultimately by man's lack of spiritual and physical companionship with his surroundings. People have not behaved properly, and God has punished them to remind them of their responsibilities. I asked Saalih why rain had not fallen for so many years prior to 1984, and he answered, "Because people are doing bad things: the Arabs, the peasants, all of us. It is said that long ago, the Palestinians—or some of them—turned their backs on religion. This is the most forbidden thing! Now look: they have no country. There are those among us too who are sinners."

The Bedouins believe that man has done too much for himself at the expense of other living things and in defiance of God. The "king of death" is responsible for an ominous trend only he can reverse, through more righteous thinking and wiser management of the environment.

7. Conservation and Conservatism

Pastoral nomads are widely regarded as being uninterested in protecting their natural resources. While they may inadvertently be in balance with their environment as long as pastures are plentiful, they make no effort to safeguard resources during times of stress, or to ensure that future generations will enjoy what nature provides. "Nomadic pastoralism is inherently self-destructive, since systems of management are based on the short-term objective of keeping as many animals as possible alive, without regard to the long-term conservation of land resources" (Allan 1976, 321). An authority on pastoralists wrote in a similar vein that the nomad attributes "no value" to improved environment, having "no vested interest in the land his flocks graze. He is not even interested in conservation. Traditionally he would scorn the idea that his flocks were overgrazing his territory. If the pasture deteriorated he would move on" (Spooner 1973, 37).[1] Khushmaan uses of plants and animals suggest exactly the opposite conclusion: pastoral nomads are exceptionally protective of their environment and work to maintain a balance between themselves, their herds, and wild resources.

Conservation Practices

The Khushmaan way of life is always in jeopardy. The principal resource supporting the nomads' desert livelihood is one that they have no control over, rainfall. The Arabs have seen drought force many of their kinspeople to give up nomadic life permanently, and they recognize that if drought persists relentlessly in the future, eventually no nomads will remain. I asked Saalih whether there would be any Khushmaan people in the desert many years from now:

It depends upon the weather. Right now there is some pasture. But if twelve or fifteen years pass without rain, we will be driven to the villages. If it rains, you'll find more of us in the mountains. Some Khushmaan children whose fathers are in towns will never know the mountains, and can walk only two or three kilometers before they tire, instead of the twenty kilometers we walk. If they don't know the plants, for example, they never will. People born in the village never change to the life of the mountains, but the reverse happens often. . . . So who will remain? After seventy years there may be no Arabs here. People will be saying, "A long time ago, my grandfather was in the mountains; we are the Arabs of the mountains." If you come after one hundred years, ask for a guide to Jebel Shaayib, you might not find one.

Remarkably, their careful use of perennial trees is one of the nomads' principal means of maintaining their traditional life-style during prolonged drought. The Bedouins recognize that if they do not molest them, perennial resources such as acacias can survive a drought of at least twelve to fifteen years' duration. These trees produce green leaves that can sustain livestock when no other pasture is available. During drought, however, there are strong temptations to overuse this perennial resource, for example, by cutting green limbs rather than shaking foliage from them. In times of environmental stress, then, the nomads must achieve a very delicate balance between using and abusing their perennial resources. The Arabs know the variables involved in this balance. They are aware of the long-term consequences of short-term gains, like hunting Barbary sheep to extinction. They know the limitations of specific plants and animals:

A *sant* [*Acacia nilotica,* a native of the Nile Valley] becomes mature in ten or twelve years, but a *sayaal* does not: it might only after fifty years. The *sayaal* does not just spring up; like the date palm, it needs a long time to grow. And it might live for a thousand years! The one Subhi cut might have been two, three, even five hundred years old. The date palm brings fruit five or six years after planting. But not the *sayaal!* And maybe after ten years the *sayaal* won't have grown back what it lost to a man's knife to feed his camels just once.

The Khushmaan now have so few perennial trees that they regard each as priceless. They know they are only a few swings of the ax away from eliminating this "drought insurance," their buffer against economic and cultural losses. They recognize that the only course of action to ensure their long-term well-being is to minimize their impact on these resources, to conserve them while using them.

Since the 1950s, when prolonged drought, excessive tree cutting, and overhunting reduced the Khushmaan resource base to a level the nomads regarded as critical, the Arabs have managed their perennial plants and game very carefully. Their conservation rules are defined clearly. The most important is that under no circumstance may green tree limbs or entire trees be cut. Only when no other food is available should a man take acacia or other tree leaves for his herd, and only then by shaking them off with his camel staff. This prohibition, which may be rooted in an understanding of the tree's ecological and economic importance, is justified by a religious explanation: God, the nomads say, demanded in the Koran that man should not cut living trees. No such reference actually exists in the Koran, and this seems to be an example of people modifying, perhaps unintentionally, what they accept as orthodoxy to suit their everyday secular needs.

As if to guarantee that trees will not be cut even if this divine prohibition should fail, the Khushmaan cite additional restrictions. The one that accounts for the protection of the greatest number of trees is the acknowledgment by all the clan that trees in particular areas may not be harmed. These protected areas are products of the bonds that individuals, families, and lineages have established with particular places (a process related in chap. 5). Even in the best of times, when annual pasture is abundant, a family prefers a certain district and will return there as often as possible. During prolonged drought the family often retires to this place to pasture livestock on perennial shrubs and acacia leaves. Apparently, as early as eighty years ago, when they first foresaw the long-term effects of tree cutting, the nomads began to make proclamations to protect trees on a family-by-family, place-by-place, basis. These founders' direct male descendants and thus, ultimately, an entire lineage becomes responsible for guaranteeing continued protection.[2]

A good example of the origin and effectiveness of this kind of protection is the "lineage preserve" founded by a man named ʿAwda at Umm Yasaar, a drainage of Jebel Gattaar. Established around 1900, it is now the premier showcase of acacia trees in Khushmaan territory: "ʿAwda, father of Sulimaan ʿAwda, declared: 'No man should come to Umm Yasaar to cut these trees for charcoal.' Now, there are a thousand acacias here. Still, no one comes here to cut, out of respect for ʿAwda, even though he has been dead for a long time. ʿAwda was a big man, who loved acacias and other plants."

Patrilineal descendants have inherited the responsibilities claimed by their ancestors. ʿAbd al-Dhaahir Sulimaan and his brothers, the paternal grandsons of ʿAwda, now patrol Umm Yasaar, for example. Suwaylim ʿAwaad established a preserve in Wadi ad-Dibb and another in Wadi Abu Haadh; his sons ʿAli and ʿAwaad and grandsons ʿIyd, Saalih, Salmaan, and Raashid are the heir-stewards of these places. Among Tababna clanspeople, ʿAli Salaama was an energetic resource protector. Around Jebel Ghaarib, he created the preserves of Umm Yasaar, Umm Fashkha,

Ghaarib, and Umm Dhaayih, and another in remote Wadi al-Hawashiyya. 'Ayd Sulimaan, son of 'Ali's paternal uncle, now monitors these. Today, such "lineage preserves," having been established over a period of several decades, account for the protection of all significant groves of trees in Khushmaan territory. Even the richest of these do not encompass great numbers of trees; the average protected area has perhaps fifty acacias.

The Khushmaan nomad has another means to protect an individual tree: he "autographs" it, declaring it must not be cut, much as does the patron of a grove of trees in a lineage preserve. To protect a rare *Rhus tripartita* tree, for example, the Khushaymi Salaama Suwaylim "autographed" it with his clan's signature: "On Jebel Ghaarib, he found a young *'irn*, and built a rock wall around it, and marked the tree with the Khushmaan *wasm*. This was about twenty years before his death in 1962. No one would dare to touch it." Another autographed tree is Ruwa'iy's Acacia (Sayaalat Ruwa'iy), one of the "living landmarks" discussed in chapter 5. Most isolated, individual acacias and other trees in Khushmaan territory are accounted for in this fashion.

Some trees are protected because of their rarity or perceived historical importance. Examples of the latter are the four crown-of-thorns trees (*sidr, Zizyphus spina-Christi*) growing in symmetrical formation around the Roman way station of Dayr Umm Sidr on the Via Porphyrites. Cairo University botanists confirmed the plausibility of the Bedouins' argument that the trees date to Roman times, even though scientists' and nomads' time scales differ. A Bedouin asked me how long these trees live. I told him I did not know; what did he think? "Maybe they are 400,000 years old; maybe that's when the Romans were here. These are the oldest trees in our countryside, the originals. It is not possible that anyone would cut their branches, because they are antiquities [*asaar*]."

In sum, the Khushmaan have three redundant and reinforcing rules that protect their trees: no tree anywhere should be cut; groups of trees within particular areas should not be cut; and specified individual trees should not be cut. The nomads' compliance with their homespun laws yielded results in the 1980s. In Wadi Gattaar, for example, Saalih perceived a revival of acacias: "In 1970 there were fewer *sayaal*. Twenty or thirty years from now, there will be plenty, if the rain is good, and if people don't cut them."

Guidelines similar to those for tree conservation apply to certain shrubs. Although they fetch high prices in Nile markets, plants such as argel and wormwood must never be uprooted or defoliated completely. The collector may prune them, leaving enough foliage or seeds to ensure new growth. He should not recrop a bush before it recovers, and within a small area he should leave some individuals of the species untouched. Finally, although there is no danger of an extensive brush fire, the Khushmaan are exceptionally careful to extinguish cooking fires before retiring or breaking camp, so as to prevent even a single shrub or tree from being burned.

The nomads apply similar principles but different methods in managing game. They have a consensus on what constitutes a reasonable take. A man should hunt infrequently, and then kill no more than one or two animals. It might seem that the nomads' rudimentary hunting technology of rocks and dogs would preclude animal overkill, but it does not. By hunting with dogs more frequently and by using the surefire palm wheel trap at water sources, people could certainly cause local extinction of ibex and greatly reduce gazelle populations. From having hunted Barbary sheep to local extinction, the Khushmaan learned of the irreversible effects of their actions. They do not want the same fate for ibex and gazelles, so they exercise moderation.

Khushmaan conservation practices are not readily apparent to the outside observer. Restraint is the principal method: daily "nonactivities" like not cutting and not charcoaling trees, not uprooting shrubs, and not overhunting game are the main conservation activities of the Khushmaan. Individuals are constantly tempted to misuse resources. Amid many *markh* (*Leptadenia pyrotechnica*) or other green trees, a man must ignore this potential source of fuel and scrounge for camel dung or dig up roots of dead plants such as *silli* (*Zilla spinosa*), rather than cut a live bough. If only green plants are available, the Arab does not burn these, even for the obligatory ritual of serving tea to the guest. Instead, the host apologizes, "There's no firewood."

For all their successes the Khushmaan are not perfect, and individuals sometimes overstep accepted boundaries of environmental behavior. Subhi ʿAwaad, for example, charcoaled two live acacias in the lineage preserve his father had established in Wadi Gattaar. Subhi was responsible for preventing such incidents in the wadi. Saalih was the first to discover what Subhi had done, and he related the details to fellow clansmen, including the Khushmaan *shaykh*. All were enraged: besides abusing his authority in the lineage preserve, Subhi had violated a clan resource. They called him, as they had when he killed a hyrax at Gattaar, names such as "dope," "beast," "criminal," "son of a dog," and "bastard." Another Khushaymi transgressor earned similar scorn from Saalih:

I became angry with Umtayr Salaama and made battle with him. To feed his camels, he had chopped off several large, green limbs from the crown of a *sayaal*. I told him, "This is forbidden!" [*haraam*]. Those trees in Wadi al-Atrash are supposed to be protected by the sons of ʿAwaad Saliim, but these men are "finished." They are not giving the *sayaal* any protection. Look at Subhi! Wasn't he supposed to protect

the *sayaal* trees of Wadi Gattaar, and instead cut them down and charcoaled them?

Between clansmen, verbal tongue-lashing like this is usually sufficient to
ensure that the individual will do no further harm; therefore, no punish-
ment is needed, and civil authorities are never consulted.

Reprimanding a violator from another clan is more difficult. In one case
Khushmaan men convened over the problem of what they called an Umsayri "crime" in their territory. To harvest ben-seeds in Wadi Abu Harba,
an Umsayri had used his camel stick to break rather than shake ben-tree
branches. The Khushmaan men lamented that these trees would not bear
fruit the following year. As this problem involved two clans, the Khushmaan men related the incident to their *shaykh,* who then rebuked his Umsayri counterpart for his clansman's misdeed.

The nomads are relatively powerless to chastise non-Bedouin offenders.
Egyptian railway workers once cut down a huge acacia in Wadi Samna.
Angry Khushmaan men urged Samna's Umsayri *shaykh* to convene a council (*majlis*) with the provincial Egyptian government. The Umsayri headman was supposed to have asked Red Sea Governorate officials to meet
with railway authorities and demand that their employees not repeat this
offense. The matter was never resolved because the *shaykh* did not act. His
apathy angered the Khushmaan.

When hunters from Qatar massacred gazelles in Khushmaan territory,
some of the nomads complained directly to officials of the Red Sea Governorate. The governorate in 1981 had passed strict laws, printed boldly on all
desert passes, prohibiting desert hunting, tree cutting, and charcoaling
and threatening poachers with six-month jail sentences and fines of $375
(300 £E). These regulations wisely exempted hunting by local Bedouins
who used traditional methods. The authorities could have reprimanded or
even punished the poachers, and in one case they turned away a would-be
hunter from Qatar. However, sportsmen usually circumvent the ban either
by bringing unquestionable permits from higher authorities in Cairo or by
obtaining provincial permits after citing purposes other than hunting for
their visits. By the time violations are brought to the attention of local officials, the hunters are long gone.

The Khushmaan have learned that the best conservation measure is to
refuse to negotiate with outsiders who want to hunt. After their experience with the Qatari hunters, some of the nomads were solicited on very
generous terms as guides by Kuwaiti hunters. The Arabs declined the
offers, telling the foreigners that there were no gazelles or ibex in the interior. I was once asked to cooperate in a similar confidence. A Khushaymi
took me to his "secret" place, a remote spring where exceptional numbers

of ibex drink, and asked me not to tell a soul where we had seen the animals.[3]

Perspectives on Bedouin Conservation

Two different but complementary ways of appreciating Khushmaan conservation practices are to relate what they mean to the nomads themselves and to suggest what outsiders may learn from the nomads about improving human relationships with the desert environment.

The Khushmaan are explicit about the purposes of their conservation practices. Their stated goals are very different from those of scientific range managers. Their practices are meant to preserve not only some economic commodities or aesthetic resources but an entire way of life: having herds, rearing children, enjoying reunions with kin, visiting special places, and practicing the freedoms they value. They recognize that unless they protect their resources this desert way of life will be lost. Saalih stated this proposition clearly: "Charcoaling is prohibited among us because without the trees, there are no animals, and no Arabs."

Conservation of plants and animals is an expression of the nomads' deep-seated conservatism. If they lost their livelihood, they would lose their desert home and their rewarding ties to particular places within it. The strong kinship bonds necessary for making a living in the desert, along with the spiritual values associated with nomadic life, would be lost. There would be an exodus of families to the Nile Valley and the Red Sea towns, where the nomads would become peasants, whom they view as their antithesis. The desert Khushmaan know this can happen: they have seen entire Maᶜaza clans and some of their own families settle down and take on peasant ways. The nomads believe that adoption of peasant ways is final and fatal. Wise use of resources is their means of avoiding this outcome. Their time frame for maintaining a desert livelihood through careful resource management extends far into the future. One man had this perspective: "Those who cut the *sayaal* trees were like animals, not thinking about the future. Today, there is no such problem. The problem would be in the future, if we do not think now."

The Bedouins have a more holistic appreciation of resources than Westerners do. They do not isolate discrete social, ecological, or spatial reasons why particular plants and animals are valuable. Instead, they wish to maintain relationships with plants and animals which are indivisible from the overall Bedouin way of life. These relationships comprise the intricate, value-laden meanings of the plants and animals which non-Bedouins view merely as "natural" resources.

Like the resources themselves, the nomads' decisions about using them are not based on exclusively ecological, social, or spatial interests. The acacia tree Sayaalat Ruwaʿiy serves as an example. Although a tree, Sayaalat Ruwaʿiy is not a "natural resource" in the Western sense. By mentioning Ruwaʿiy's Acacia, the nomad commemorates Ruwaʿiy the man. At the same time he refers to the desert's most useful tree species. Finally, Sayaalat Ruwaʿiy not only has a location but is a locus: "*huwa huwa*," the Arabs say of such things, "It is it." If asked whether he protects Sayaalat Ruwaʿiy because it is a tree, a place, or a personal monument, the Arab might answer, "It is it."

For outsiders the most notable feature of Khushmaan conservation may be that it exists at all, in view of the negative perceptions of nomads' relationships with environment. More important, this indigenous conservation system also holds practical implications for resource management on a broader scale. There is growing interest among international conservationists, development planners, and scholars in what has been called "folk ecology" and "ethnoconservation" (Richards 1975; Pitt 1985). These authorities contend that traditional peoples often have profound and detailed knowledge of their ecosystems and effective ways of using them sustainably. Furthermore, they insist, traditional environmental knowledge and resource management practices provide an alternative basis for conservation and development which may be superior to what Western science and know-how offer.[4]

Working with these ideas, development and conservation agents have applied the traditional know-how and techniques of farmers, fishers, and hunters to specific projects in sub-Saharan Africa, the southwest Pacific, and the Arctic. However, until now they have not applied the traditional knowledge of pastoral nomads for similar purposes in arid lands. The main reason may be that many authorities have been convinced by the argument that nomads are reckless environmental "pirates."

Another factor that might dissuade conservation and development authorities from considering Bedouin conservation as a basis for action is the belief that traditional systems only coincidentally protect the environment. Margaret Chapman discussed the importance of this issue:

> Some traditional groups not only possess an acute awareness of the environment and an ability to exploit its resources efficiently, but they are also knowledgeable conservationists. However, here one must distinguish between those groups who apply conservation measures intentionally to prevent resource depletion, and those whose various cultural beliefs and rituals inadvertently serve to conserve resources. . . . Intentional conservation measures are particularly interesting, as those groups which apply them show that rare quality in human societies—

an awareness of the finiteness of their environment. Also, to know which conservation measures to apply, and when and where to do it, such people must be particularly skilled in picking up and interpreting environmental "cues" which indicate the possibility of an imbalance developing between population and resources. (1985, 217)

The Khushmaan do conserve their resources intentionally, and their practices draw from detailed knowledge of the desert ecosystem. It may be useful to indicate some specific ways in which the Khushmaan and perhaps other nomads could be consulted as environmental experts. First, they can offer biologists a nearly complete basic inventory of their region's plants, animals, and other resources; this is typically the starting point for any environmental project. The Khushmaan know at least 155 plant species, of which I was, with their assistance, able to collect 147, far more than had been recognized previously by botanists in the area. Second, the nomads offer insights into ecology that trained scientists lack the time and resources to observe in the field. Of each of their 155-plus plant species, for example, the Khushmaan know habitats; distributions; life cycles; medicinal uses; palatability for man, livestock, and wild animals; usefulness as fuel; and other qualities. Third, they know the extent to which they can exploit a given species before diminishing its ability to recover. This knowledge guides their conservation practices, which could be adopted or encouraged by outside experts. Fourth, the nomads could suggest if an already-planned project for conservation or development in their area would succeed and could recommend modifications that would help it succeed. Finally, they could propose appropriate interventions, for example, by suggesting that planting acacias would be a wise use of funds and manpower designated for environmental improvement.

The traditional knowledge and skills of pastoral nomads, developed over thousands of years of experience with the desert, should be of priority interest to Egypt and other arid nations with severe environmental problems. Egyptian experts, for example, have long recognized that the deserts represent a major potential for alleviating the overcrowding and resource shortages plaguing their country. One handicap that prevents this goal from being realized is the belief that experts must start from scratch to discover what resources the deserts offer. Another is the Nile-dwellers' deep-rooted anxieties about human abilities to work and live in deserts. In both cases the nomads have much to offer. Ironically, despite their forward-looking ambitions about the desert environment, the Egyptians' greatest handicap may be their refusal, based on their outmoded perceptions of nomads as lawless, destructive vagabonds, to seek help from the Bedouin experts. In an article entitled "Why the Antagonistic Attitude towards the

Deserts and How to Overcome the Situation," the Egyptian author, while lamenting the poverty of information on how people might harvest the desert, bars pastoralists from making any contributions:

> Availability of studies on natural resources and how to be developed in deserts will be an attraction for the youth who will get to know that there is something to deal with and something to develop. Such information should also be common to people living in the desert who speak for the natural resources, for ways and means to overcome difficulties met in the desert and apparently will be the backbone of any project in the desert including any public awareness project. In that respect, we do not talk about pastoralism since loyalty to the state and obedience to its legislation, law and order, nationalism and modern education can only be achieved with sedentary population. Meanwhile, tent dwelling nomads require firewood rather than other fuels for cooking and heating, and collect this by felling bush and trees along their routes of migration leading by the end to desertification. (Ali 1978, 10)

My point is not that all pastoral nomads are in perfect harmony with their environments or that they always offer the best possible means of achieving such harmony; there are numerous examples to the contrary. Instead, the Khushmaan example points to the need for much more basic research on nomads' relations with environment and to the need to reevaluate long-standing beliefs about nomads held by Western anthropologists, ecologists, and experts on nomadism and by national governments and sedentary inhabitants of the countries in which nomads live. Critics of nomads' resource uses who are all too aware of the obvious abuses should look also for what cannot readily be seen, the kind of "nonactivities" for conservation described above. The fact that pastoral nomadism has been practiced successfully for nearly ten thousand years recommends that this way of life be studied very carefully.

One reason why Bedouin conservation efforts exceed outsiders' low expectations is that these expectations are based on faulty assumptions about some basic nomad-environment relationships. The Khushmaan example suggests that long-standing views of the resource base, spatial affinities, and social identity of nomads should be reconsidered.

The first assumption that Khushmaan experience challenges is that pastoral nomads rely solely upon annual or ephemeral pasture, the drought-avoiding resources which occur randomly in time and space whenever and wherever rain falls. However, there is another vital set of resources which the Khushmaan harvest in the desert, especially when rain fails: perennial plants and those animals which endure long-term drought.

Second, the Khushmaan defy the expected pattern of nomads' relations with the spatial environment. The corollary to the belief that nomads rely only on annual pasture is that pastoral nomadism is exclusively a drought-avoiding livelihood, in which migration to ephemeral drought-avoiding resources is the only means of survival. It is widely believed that when annual plants fail to appear for a long period over the entire area in which a given nomadic group makes its living, that group must either become sedentary or pursue wage labor and other activities outside the desert. However, the Khushmaan have another adaptation to prolonged drought. During these periods they become almost nonnomadic, using perennial resources in limited areas for long periods of time. Their adaptation is to endure drought, like the adaptation of the resources they use at such times. Notably, in protecting these "fixed" resources, individuals are protecting small areas dear to them, which contradicts the notion that they are "placeless" and therefore inclined to abuse common property.

Finally, Khushmaan conservation reveals that the nomad's identity is far more individualistic than is generally supposed. Individuals, their families, and lineages pledge their personalities and small collective identities to particular places and the resources which occur in them. This appears to contradict the ideology expressed by most Bedouin groups, including the Khushmaan themselves, which insists that all individuals in the clan and tribe are equal with respect to use of places and access to resources. On closer examination Khushmaan conservation practices seem to be effective because individuals do in fact work to uphold the common interests of the clan. This refutes many scholars' argument that individual nomads abuse resources because they cannot live up to communal obligations.

The nomads are not, as many believe them to be, unwitting servants of nature's whims. They are people who make choices in order to cope with environmental extremes. The Khushmaan apparently have had to innovate in order to protect their resource base because their ideal of common access to resources could not guarantee sustainable resource use during times of prolonged drought. If their ideology, which regards all places and biotic resources as common property of all the clan, were sufficient even in the worst drought, there would be no need for individuals to assert their own identities; in keeping with clan spirit no one would misuse the "commons." Since 1900, however, as the collective wealth of clan resources has declined while droughts have been particularly severe, individuals, families, and lineages have assumed increasing responsibilities for resources in particular places. In view of the nomads' abilities to adapt themselves to some of the world's most marginal conditions, this innovation is not surprising.

Conclusion

While traveling with the Khushmaan, I often felt that my companions hailed from an earlier time. Both the modern and ancient people of these mountains possessed simple things made from hide, wood, and stone. They cooked ibex in the same style of rock oven and hunted these animals in the same manner. A few years ago in a rock shade in Wadi Umm Haadh, some Khushmaan men scrawled a scene of an ibex chase. They worked alongside an almost identical scene etched by an ancient hunter perhaps six thousand years earlier.

Antiquities weather very slowly in the Khushmaan desert, so the Bedouins feel close to the past. History plays an active role in their daily lives. When we wanted tea but had no fuel on Jebel Abu Dukhaan, Saalih retired to a Roman blacksmith's shop to retrieve some ancient charcoal. He marveled at the apparently fresh footprint of a man who worked gold at Ras as-Saagia almost two thousand years ago. The miner had been washing native rock to separate ore when he stepped into this solution, leaving his signature. At a hermit's cave in the South Galala Plateau, Saalih ran his fingers reverently down the furrows in plaster made by the holy man's hand sixteen hundred years ago. Later he led me to a secret spot where a four-foot-high Roman amphora stands in perfect condition: secret because the Bedouins want to protect their past from irreverent hands and eyes.

On Jebel Abu Dukhaan, Saalih remarked about local history: "The Romans left, the ibex stayed." Sulimaan Suwaylim, Saalih's uncle, had said almost the same thing to his way-fellow Leo Tregenza in 1951: "The Romans went, and the ibexes came" (1958, 163). Such enduring perceptions reveal how little the conditions and beliefs of the nomads have changed during decades of tumult and technological revolution elsewhere. The Bedouins have not followed the currents of the twentieth century, not because these have not reached them but because the nomads have had the collective self-confidence and pride of place and livelihood to resist the world offered by radio, television, shiny tin, and gaudy cloth. In one hundred years another foreigner may be led down the same desert pathways that Leo Tregenza and I followed, to learn the same time-proven Bedouin ways of seeing things.

Drought could prevent this. So could the short-sightedness of people who do not appreciate the nomads' way of living with their surroundings. Some observers feel that there is no place for such an ancient way of life in the modern world: "pastoral nomadism has become an anachronism, and, as such, is destined for extinction," wrote one (Mikesell 1970, 46). Some believe that this process of extinction should be assisted by enticing or forcing nomads to settle. Still others believe that pastoral nomadism will have to be reformed: "the most important conclusion with regard to the future of pastoral nomadism is that if it is to survive as a way of life and a method of production, outside intervention becomes inevitable" (Konczacki 1978, 36).

Instead of insisting that nomads settle, or assuming that their livelihood is faulty and in need of outside management, we might look to groups like the Khushmaan for instruction on how to use desert resources more wisely. For some ten thousand years, only pastoral nomads have made a successful, sustainable living in some of earth's most difficult places. In a world of expanding deserts, there is much to learn from them.

Appendix 1   Bedouin, Latin, and English Plant and Animal Names

This list follows the Khushmaan classification of plants and animals. It is the most complete inventory I could compile, and there are many gaps which need to be filled.

Each plant or animal is listed first by its Khushmaan name. Below this is the vernacular English name (if available; most plants have none) and/or the number (if any) of the specimen collected. The Linnaean name is given in the next column. Not all specimens have been keyed to the level of genus and species, and some specimens collected have still not been identified. Several species for which the Khushmaan have names have not yet been collected. Some (Linnaean) species have no Khushmaan name; thus "none" appears where the Khushmaan name would. These generally are plants and animals which I collected in the Galala and other districts that the Khushmaan seldom visit, including mountain summits.

Specimen numbers for plants refer to the author's collection deposited at the Herbarium of the National Research Center in Dokki, Egypt. I am grateful to Dr. Loutfy Boulos and his student Loutfy Mohsen for these identifications. Specimen numbers for animals refer to a separate collection I deposited with Steven Goodman at the University of Michigan Museum of Zoology. Goodman identified some of these and distributed others for further examination. In particular I thank Dr. Mark O'Brien of the Museum of Zoology, University of Michigan, for identifying the reptiles, and Dr. David Furth of the Peabody Museum, Yale University, for keying the insects. I am also grateful to Dr. Harry Hoogstraal and the staff of Medical Zoology at the U.S. Naval Medical Research Unit No. 3 in Cairo for accepting and identifying my collection of ectoparasites. In the 1940s Leo Tregenza identified most of the Khushmaan birds, including the difficult warblers. Latin names for the birds follow the systematic list of Goodman, Meininger, Baha El Din, Hobbs, and Mullie (1988). Mammal names are provided by Osborn and Helmy (1980); reptile names, by Marx (1968); and plant names, by Tackholm (1974).

NABAATAAT: THE PLANT "KINGDOM"

aahina
no specimen

ʿadaam
    225, 256   *Ephedra alata*

adhbah
    87, 121   *Scorzonera schweinfurthii*

adh-hayaan
    no specimen

ʿaguul
    65   *Alhagi graecorum*

akhala
    no specimen

albayna
    152   *Euphorbia granulata*

ʿalda
    1   *Ephedra aphylla*

ʿanab adh-dhiib
    18, 302   *Solanum nigrum*

ʿaraad
    88, 267   *Salsola vermiculata*

araak
    64   *Salvadora persica*

araymba
    115   *Bassia eriophora*

arbayaan
    290, 321   *Cotula cinerea*

arta
    14   *Calligonum comosum*

asfayr adh-dhaan (ʿibaysi)
    161   *Cleome chrysantha*

asfiiʿa
    148   *Senecio flavus*

ʿaslaa
    90, 254   *Suaeda monoica*

athgar
    168   *Morettia philaena*

athl
    218   *Tamarix aphylla*
    5   *Tamarix amplexicaulis*

ʿawshiz
    293, 158, 316   *Lycium shawii*

ʿaylijaan
    114   *Pituranthos tortuosus*

ʿaysilaan (bisayl)
   56   *Colchicum* sp.

baʿaytharaan
   13   *Artemisia judaica*

bawrag
   133   *Asphodelus fistulosus*

birkaan
   81   *Centaurea scoparia*

bisayl (ʿaysilaan)
   56   *Colchicum* sp.

bruubi
   273, 219   *Typha domingensis*

burrayd (zaʿytamaan)
   no specimen

butm
   45   *Pistacia khinjuk*

daʿaa-a
   159   *Aizoon canariense*

dahamii
   277   *Erodium glaucophyllum*

dalsam
   187   *Taverniera aegyptiaca*

dhafara
   80   *Iphiona mucronata*

dhanaba dhabb
   137   *Blepharis ciliaris*

dharagrag
   177   *Trigonella stellata*

dharamit ad-daar
   no specimen

dharamit al-himaar
   10, 287   *Salvia aegyptiaca*

dharamit an-nuur
   no specimen

dhaynabaan
   60, 298   *Caylusea hexagyna*
   84   *Telephium sphaerospermum*

fashkha
   31, 131   *Cocculus pendulus*

faynii
   167, 320   *Arnebia hispidissima*

firs
165, 215   Salsola baryosma

gadhiim
275   *Helianthemum lipii*
102   *Helianthemum kahiricum*

gadhub
178   *Lotus deserti*

garayn
no specimen

garmal
171   *Zygophyllum simplex*

garnaa
109   *Monsonia heliotropoides*

gataf
107   *Atriplex leucoclada*

gatub
208   *Tribulus* sp.

gaysuum
76   *Achillea fragrantissima*

ghaaba
91, 296, 248, 313   *Phragmites australis*
172, 180

ghaaga
271, 301   *Astragalus sieberi*

ghadha
106   *Haloxylon persicum*

ghardag
2   *Nitraria retusa*

ghaylga
138   *Pergularia tomentosa*

gilaygila
113   *Isatis microcarpa*
118   *Pteranthus dichotomus*

gilu
110   *Anabasis setifera*

gimayh (gutbi gamh)
217, 123   *Astragalus vogelii*

giray^c a
no specimen   *Papaver decaisnei?*

gutbi faga^c aa
125   *Astragalus eremophilus*

guurdhi
    160   *Ochradenus baccatus*

haadh
    85   *Cornulaca monacantha*

hadhaaᶜa
    282   *Lasiurus hirsutus*

hajnii
    92   *Aeluropus littoralis*
    297a   *Aeluropus massauensis*

half
    265, 325, 184, 39   *Imperata cylindrica*
    236   *Polypogon monspeliensis*

hamdh
    59   *Salsola schweinfurthii*

hammaat
    40, 202   *Ficus pseudosycomorus*

handhal
    66   *Citrullus colocynthis*

handhal al-ghazaal
    27   *Cucumis prophetarum*

haraaz
    22   *Acacia albida*

harjal
    41   *Solenostemma arghel*

harjal adh-dhiib (harjal hadhari)
    57, 294, 144   *Gomphocarpus sinaicus*

harra
    120, 242, 257, 281   *Diplotaxis harra*

hasaad
    329 (lost)   *Crypsis schoenoides?*
                         Astenantherum forsskalei?

hashiish
    42, 49   *Stipagrostis plumosa*

hidayda
    82   *Zygophyllum album*

himaadh
    142   *Rumex vesicarius*

hurbith
    157, 326   *Lotononis platycarpa*

huwwi
    71, 240   *Launaea nudicaulis*

huwwi tiiz al-kalba (Dharamit
    al-kalb, nugud)
    24, 156   *Reichardia tingitana*
    285   *Launaea cassiniana*

ʿibaysi (asfayr adh-dhaan)
    161   *Cleome chrysantha*

idhn al-faar
    176   *Parietaria alsinifolia*

igbaydha
    189   *Anastatica hierochuntica*

ikhnaana
    153   *Plantago ovata*

ikhzaama
    9, 26   *Reseda pruinosa*

ʿiliig
    249   *Oxystelma alpinii*

irgayga
    186   *Robbairea delileana*
    260   *Paronychia arabica*

ʿirn
    unnumbered   *Rhus tripartita*

ishkaaʿa
    219, 166   *Fagonia thebaica*

ʿishrig
    no specimen

ithmaam
    283, 191   *Panicum turgidum*

jaʿaada
    126, 203, 211   *Teucrium leucocladum*

jamba
    135   *Fagonia bruguieri*

jarad
    201, 220   *Gymnocarpos decandrum*
    269   *Halogeton alopecuroides*

jaraybii
    79   *Farsetia aegyptia*
    324   *Farsetia ramosissima*

jithaath
    140   *Francoeria crispa*

kaddas
    96, 33, 207   *Scrophularia deserti*

kahalii
   101   *Anchusa milleri*
khariit
   129   *Salsola baryosma*
khashiir
   311   *Echinops glaberrimus*
   274   *Echinops spinosus*
khibb
   199, 247   not identifiable
khubayz
   70, 322   *Malva parviflora*
   28   *Althaea ludwigii*
   111   *Erodium pulverulentum*
khushirif
   73   *Centaurea eryngioides*
kibaath
   50, 162   *Launea spinosa*
kidaad
   104   *Astragalus spinosus*
lassaf
   209   *Capparis cartilaginea*
laysuuf
   119, 228   *Capparis spinosa*
lijliij
   192   *Balanites aegyptiaca*
lissaak
   124   *Forskholea tenacissima*
mahad
   174   *Schouwia thebaica*
makur
   30   *Polycarpaea repens*
markh
   4   *Leptadenia pyrotechnica*
mashta
   12   *Cleome droserifolia*
masruur
   54   *Cynomorium coccineum*
mayshii
   62, 239   f: *Umbelliferae*
muliih
   94, 136, 258   *Reaumuria hirtella*

murghayd
116   *Erodium glaucophyllum*

najiil
6   *Cynodon dactylon*

nakhl
date palm   *Phoenix dactylifera*

nassi
122   *Poa sinaica*

natash
35, 183   *Crotalaria aegyptiaca*

niila
181, 190   *Chrozophora oblongifolia*

numsaa
38, 235, 173   *Juncus rigidus*

rabl
8   *Pulicaria undulata*

rahaab
139   *Heliotropium arbainense*

ratam
93   *Retam raetam*

rayl
188   *Aerva javanica*
63   *Stachys aegyptiaca*

rimth
164   *Haloxylon salicornicum*

rughl
175   *Atriplex inamoena*
234   *Atriplex dimorphostegia*

rutrayt
7   *Zygophyllum coccineum*

saᶜdaan
284   *Neurada procumbens*

salam
34   *Acacia ehrenbergiana*

sanna
204   *Cassia italica*

sant (cultivated)
53   *Acacia nilotica*

sarh
145   *Maerua crassifolia*

sawaas
46, 206   *Periploca aphylla*

sayaal
   23, 195   *Acacia raddiana*
saykaraan
   48, 318   *Hyoscyamus boveanus*
shawra
   252   *Avicennia marina*
shaykuuʿa
   85   *Fagonia tristis*
shaykuuʿa abu riiha
   108   *Fagonia arabica*
shibrim
   unnumbered   *Convolvulus hystrix*
shiih
   103   *Artemisia herba-alba*
shiʿirgaan
   20, 185, 303   *Adiantum capillus-veneris*
shugaar
   117   *Matthiola livida*
sidr
   298c, 98   *Zizyphus spina-Christi*
silli
   43   *Zilla spinosa*
sirr
   55   *Noaea mucronata*
summaa
   130   *Silene linearis*
suwayd
   278   *Rhamnus dispermus*
tarfa
   51, 214, 253, 232   *Tamarix nilotica*
thilaathi
   61   *Seidlitzia rosmarinus*
   300   *Halogeton alopeluroides*
tumayr
   100   *Erodium hirtum*
tundhub
   83, 216   *Capparis decidua*
ʿujirim
   105   *Anabasis articulata*
umm jayniina
   150, 299   *Cleome trinervia*

uraaga
179   *Fagonia mollis*

ʿushar
  unnumbered   *Calotropis procera*

yahaag
97   *Diplotaxis acris*

yahmiim
270   *Trichodesma africana*

yahmiim dhabbaani
128   *Trichodesma africana*

yasar
16, 193, 315   *Moringa peregrina*

yasliih
75   *Erucaria pinnata*

zaʿatar
72   *Thymus bovei*

zaʿytamaan
  no specimen

zayta
11   *Lavandula stricta*
276, 255   *Lavandula pubescens*

zibb adh-dhiikh
295   *Cistanche phelypaea*

zinayma
288   *Ifloga spicata*
154   *Filago prolifera*

none
229, 231   *Podonosma galalensis*

none
194   *Cometes abyssinica*

none
291   *Cleome amblyocarpa*

none
312, 306, 47, 304   *Conyza bovei*

none
264, 46   *Gnaphalium luteo-album*

none
21, 25   *Phagnalon barbeyanum*

none
74   *Sisymbrium irio*

none
268, 67   *Andrachne aspera*

none 77	*Bromus fasciculatus*
none 272	*Piptatherum miliaceum*
none 17	*Nepeta persica*
none 69	*Astragalus cruciatus*
none 52	*Tephrosia apollinea*
none 44	*Olea indica*
none 262	*Polypogon monspeliensis*
none 259, 226, 243	*Samolus valerandi*
none 317	*Rhamnus* sp. (deposited at Kew)
none 15, 32	*Kohautia caespitosa*
none 182	*Anticharis glandulosa*
none 289, 223, 224	*Kickxia aegyptiaca*
none 197, 163	*Lindenbergia indica*
none 212	*Lindenbergia sinaica*
none 86	*Hyoscyamus desertorum*
none 238	*Apium graveolens*
none 58, 292	*Peganum harmala*
none 19	*Kickxia* sp.
none 98	*Paronychia arabica*

HAYAWAANAAT: THE ANIMAL "KINGDOM"

1. *Khanziir:* Swine
   A. *Bani Aadam,* Man
   B. *Namnam* (chimpanzee) and *Silaʿawi* (gorilla), Humanlike Swine
   C. *Khanziir,* Swine Proper
      a. *Gird,* monkeys
      b. *Khanziir,* domestic pig
      c. *Himaar,* domestic donkey
      d. *Kalb,* "dogs"

     abul-husayn
       Rueppell's sand fox   *Vulpes rueppelli*
     dabʿ
       striped hyena   *Hyaena hyaena*
     dhiib
       jackal   *Canis aureus*
     gutt
       caracal   *Caracal caracal*
     kalb
       domestic dog   *Canis familiaris*
     nimr
       leopard   *Panthera pardus*
     shiib
       wolf?   *Canis lupus?*
     none
       sand cat   *Felis margarita*
      e. *Faar,* "Mice"
     faar
       lesser gerbil   *Gerbillus gerbillus*
       pigmy dipodil   *Dipodillus henleyi*
       bushy-tailed dipodil   *Sekeetamys calurus*
     abu shawk
       Egyptian spiny mouse   *Acomys cahirinus*
     jirdhi
       silky jird   *Meriones crassus*
     sibaahi
       lesser jerboa   *Jaculus jaculus*

2. *Humanlike Nonswine*
   dhabb
      Egyptian dabb-lizard   *Uromastyx aegyptius*
      eyed dabb-lizard   *Uromastyx ocellatus*
   wabr
      rock hyrax   *Procavia capensis*

3. *Hayawaanaat,* True Animals

    arnab
        Egyptian hare   *Lepus capensis*

    bill
        camel   *Camelus dromedarius*

    badan
        Nubian ibex   *Capra ibex*

    dhabi
        dorcas gazelle   *Gazella dorcas*

    ghanam
        domestic goat   *Capra hircus*

    *kabsh al-khala*a*
        Barbary sheep   *Ammotragus lervia*

    *na*aaj*
        domestic sheep   *Ovis longipes*

4. *Tayr,* Flying Creatures

    *abayd *abaar rakhaam*
        Egyptian vulture   *Neophron percnopterus*

    *abu al-*ala*
        red-backed shrike   *Lanius collurio*
        masked shrike   *Lanius nubicus*
        lesser grey shrike   *Lanius minor*
        great grey shrike   *Lanius excubitor*
        woodchat shrike   *Lanius senator*

    abu jiraab
        white pelican   *Pelecanus onocrotalus*

    adhgat
        a botfly. 43   *Oestrus ovis*

    anaz
        black stork   *Ciconia nigra*

    asbuul
        dragonflies. no specimen

    *ba*uudha*
        mosquitoes. no specimen

    buuma
        little owl   *Athene noctua*

    dabra
        wasps. 49, 21   *Pompilus vespiformis*

    dhubaab
        a fly. 32   o: *Diptera*
                            f: *Bombyliidae*

    dhubaab al-argat (min al-yasar)
        a fly. no specimen

dhubaab al-bill

I

o: *Diptera*
f: *Tabanidae*

dhubaab hamdaani

14

o: *Diptera*
f: *Calliphoridae*

firaash
   moths and butterflies. no
     specimen

firra
   common quail   *Coturnix coturnix*

fisaysi
   icterine warbler   *Hippolais icterina*
   olivaceous warbler   *Hippolais pallida*
   barred warbler   *Sylvia nisoria*
   orphean warbler   *Sylvia hortensis*
   whitethroat   *Sylvia communis*
   desert warbler   *Sylvia nana*
   Ruppell's warbler   *Sylvia rueppelli*
   Sardinian warbler   *Sylvia melanocephala*
   subalpine warbler   *Sylvia cantillans*
   spectacled warbler   *Sylvia conspicillata*
   Arabian warbler   *Sylvia leucomelaena*
   willow warbler   *Phylloscopus trochilus*
   chiffchaff   *Phylloscopus collybita*
   Bonelli's warbler   *Phylloscopus bonelli*
   streaked scrub warbler   *Scotocerca inquieta*
   spotted flycatcher   *Muscicapa striata*

garaadh
   a cricket. 48, 8   *Gryllus bimaculatus*

garaadh al-gayla
   a locust. 13

o: *Orthoptera*
f: *Acrididae*

garawaan
   cream-colored courser   *Cursorius cursor*

gataa
   spotted sandgrouse   *Pterocles senegallus*
   coronetted sandgrouse   *Pterocles coronatus*

gharag (kutub kaali)
   night heron   *Nycticorax nycticorax*

gharariyya
   European coot   *Fulica atra*

gharnuug
   cattle egret   *Egretta ibis*
   western reef heron   *Egretta gularis*

ghuraab
  brown-necked raven   *Corvus ruficollis*

giigi
  hoopoe lark   *Alaemon alaudipes*

gimriyya
  laughing dove   *Streptopelia senegalensis*
  (known from Nile Valley)

gubbaar abu fi-gafaa
  hoopoe   *Upupa epops*

hajal
  sand partridge   *Ammoperdix heyi*

hid-hid
  eagle owl   *Bubo bubo*

hubaaraa
  houbara bustard   *Chlamydotis undulata*

ihdayii
  honey buzzard   *Pernis apivorus*
  short-toed eagle   *Circaetus gallicus*
  buzzard   *Buteo buteo*
  long-legged buzzard   *Buteo rufinus*
  booted eagle   *Hieraeetus pennatus*
  Bonelli's eagle   *Hieraeetus fasciatus*
  hen-harrier   *Circus cyaneus*
  pallid harrier   *Circus macrourus*
  marsh harrier   *Circus aeruginosus*
  Montagu's harrier   *Circus pygargus*
  red kite   *Milvus milvus*
  black kite   *Milvus migrans*

irgayᶜa
  pale crag martin   *Hirundo obsoleta*
  European swallow   *Hirundo rustica*
  red-rumped swallow   *Hirundo daurica*
  house martin   *Delichon urbica*

jaᶜal
  a beetle. 33   o: *Coleoptera*
                                  f: *Scarabaeidae*

jakhdhub
  a locust. 37   *Dericorys albidula*

jakhdhub al-markh
  a locust. no specimen

jiraad
  a grasshopper. 17   o: *Orthoptera*
                                  f: *Acrididae*

kalb is-hayl
  European bee-eater   *Merops apiaster*
  blue-cheeked bee-eater   *Merops superciliosus*

kutub kaali (gharag)
  night heron   *Nycticorax nycticorax*

min al-yasar (dhubaab al-argat)
  a fly. no specimen

na‘aam
  ostrich   *Struthio camelus*

nahal
  a bee. no specimen

namuus
  a midge. 30, 57   o: *Hymenoptera*
                          f: *Chalcidoidea*

nisr
  griffon vulture   *Gyps fulvus*
  Ruppell's vulture   *Gyps ruppellii*
  lappet-faced vulture   *Gypaetus barbatus*

raahu
  white stork   *Ciconia ciconia*

raggaada
  nightjar   *Caprimulgus europaeus*
  Egyptian nightjar   *Caprimulgus aegyptius*

rahaydin
  desert lark   *Ammomanes deserti*
  bar-tailed desert lark   *Ammomanes cincturus*

rakhaam
  Egyptian vulture   *Neophron percnopterus*

ruway‘i
  gray wagtail   *Motacilla cinerea*
  white wagtail   *Motacilla alba*
  yellow wagtail   *Motacilla flava*

sagr
  sooty falçon   *Falco concolor*
  lanner falcon   *Falco biarmicus*
  peregrine falcon   *Falco peregrinus*
  Barbary falcon   *Falco pelegrinoides*
  saker falcon   *Falco cherrug*
  Eleonora's falcon   *Falco eleonorae*
  red-footed falcon   *Falco vespertinus*
  hobby   *Falco subbuteo*
  lesser kestrel   *Falco naumanni*
  kestrel   *Falco tinnunculus*
  Levant sparrowhawk   *Accipiter gentilis*
  sparrowhawk   *Accipiter nisus*

sayf rabbina
  a mantid. 46

o: *Mantodea*
f: *Mantidae*

shadhabba
  ibex fly. 3, 40, 44, 47, 54

Hippobosca pupiparcus

silaawi
  lammergeyer

Gypaetus barbatus

slaygaw
  wheatear

Oenanthe oenanthe

  mourning wheatear

Oenanthe lugens

  desert wheatear

Oenanthe deserti

  hooded wheatear

Oenanthe monacha

  white-rumped black wheatear

Oenanthe leucopyga

  pied wheatear

Oenanthe pleschanka

  isabelline wheatear

Oenanthe isabellina

  red-tailed wheatear

Oenanthe xanthroprymna

  black-eared wheatear

Oenanthe hispanica

tayr al-rabiiᶜa
  tawny pipit

Anthus campestris

  water pipit

Anthus spinoletta

  red-throated pipit

Anthus cervinus

  tree pipit

Anthus trivialis

  meadow pipit

Anthus pratensis

ᶜugaab
  lesser spotted eagle

Aquila pomarina

  steppe eagle

Aquila nipalensis

  spotted eagle

Aquila clanga

  golden eagle

Aquila chrysaetos

witwaat
  bats

Rhinopoma sp.
Pathyzos sp.

wizz ᶜiraag
  common crane

Grus grus

yimaam
  turtle dove

Streptopelia turtur

zarzuur (janzuur)
  house sparrow

Passer domesticus

  Spanish sparrow

Passer hispaniolensis

  trumpeter finch

Rhodopechys githaginea

5. *Duud,* Crawling Creatures
  aaf
    Egyptian cobra

Naja haje

  abu sayha
    Gray's agama

Agama agama spinosa

ʿagrab al-miy
  water scorpion   o: *Hemiptera*
                                   f: *Nefidae*

ʿalag
  a leach. no specimen
antabuuk
  a spider. 24   not yet identified
arabuuna
  Bosc's lizard   *Acanthodactylus boskianus*
  nidua lizard   *Acanthodactylus scutellatus*
  small-spotted lizard   *Eremias guttulata*
arbaʿa wa arbdʿiin
  a centipede. 55   o: *Chilopoda*
                                   f: *Scolupodendridae*

ʿardha
  a termite. 26   o: *Isoptera*
ashbath
  camel spider. 23.   *Galeodes arabs*
ʿayr al-banaat
  a beetle. 4, 36, 45   *Adesmia* sp.
basaaga
  camel cricket. 18   *Lezina* sp.
brays
  fan-footed gecko   *Ptychodactylus hasselquisti*
  Egyptian gecko   *Tarentola annularis*
  Steudner's gecko   *Tropiocolotes steudneri*
daffaana
  ant lion. no specimen
dalamma
  ticks (adult females). 6   *Hyalomma dromedarii*
                                   Hyalomma anatolicum

darja
  a silverfish. 35   o: *Diplura*
dhaawi
  a snake. no specimen
dharnaah
  an ant. no specimen
dharr ahmar
  an ant. 16   o: *Hymenoptera*
                                   f: *Formicidae*

dharr aswad
  an ant. 22   o: *Hymenoptera*
                                   f: *Formicidae*

dhiiba adh-dhibaan
　　a spider. 9, 56　　　　　　　　not yet identified

duud bitaaʿa rimma
　　carrion beetle (pupa). 42　　　o: *Diptera*

fash
　　ibex tick. unnumbered　　　　*Ornithodoros foleyi*

faʿuus
　　caterpillars. no specimen

faʾuus al-himaadh
　　a caterpillar. no specimen

fisaaya
　　a beetle. 5, 38　　　　　　　*Ocnera* sp.

gamla
　　gazelle louse. 15　　　　　　not yet identified

garfa
　　a "stinkbug." no specimen

guraad
　　ticks (medium-sized).　　　　*Haemphysalis sulcata*
　　　unnumbered　　　　　　　*Hyalomma dromedarii*
　　　　　　　　　　　　　　　Hyalomma anatolicum

halwizaan
　　a snail. 41　　　　　　　　　*Eremica desertorum*

hanash
　　greater cerastes viper　　　　*Cerastes cerastes*

hayya
　　ant lion. no specimen

hibayna
　　Sinai agama　　　　　　　　*Agama sinaita*
　　changeable agama　　　　　　*Agama mutabilis*

hidhif
　　Burton's carpet viper　　　　*Echis coloratus*

huuta al-maaya
　　a water beetle. no specimen

igʿays
　　an ant. 31, 20　　　　　　　o: *Hymenoptera*
　　　　　　　　　　　　　　　f: *Formicidae*

ʿith
　　a beetle. 2　　　　　　　　　*Dermestes* sp.

khumlaa
　　ticks (immature).　　　　　　*Hyalomma dromedarii*
　　　unnumbered　　　　　　　*Hyalomma anatolicum*

lukaaz
　　Audouin's sand skink　　　　*Chalcides sepsoides*

mallaja
  Eyed skink   *Chalcides ocellatus*

minn bitaaʿa as-silla
  a beetle. no specimen

murgayba
  a beetle. 10   o: *Coleoptera*
                            f: *Tenebrionidae*

nabbaala
  7   o: *Hemiptera*
                            f: *Cercopidae* or *Fulgoroidea*

nagra
  a beetle. no specimen

nahashal
  an ant. 19   o: *Hymenoptera*
                            f: *Formicidae*

nimla
  an ant. 11, 58   o: *Hymemoptera*
                            f: *Formicidae*

sayda
  lesser cerastes viper. no   *Cerastes vipera*
    specimen

sill
  Schokari sand snake   *Psammophis schokari*
  Saharan sand snake   *Psammophis aegyptius*

sill al-argat
  Jan's desert racer.   *Coluber rhodorhachis*
    unnumbered

suusa
  grain beetle. 29   o: *Coleoptera*
                            f: *Tenebrionidae*

umhayk
  a ladybug. 51   o: *Coleoptera*
                            f: *Cocinellidae*

umm Sulimaan wa Saalim
  a mantid. unnumbered   o: *Mantodea*
                            f: *Mantidae*

waral
  desert monitor. no specimen *Varanus griseus*

none
  a water snail. 50   *Bulinus truncatus*

none
  a water beetle. 53   *Potomonectes* sp.

none
  an earwig. 28   *Forficula* sp.

 a sowbug. 27   o: *Isopoda*

6. *Samak,* Swimming Creatures
 samak
  a fairy shrimp. 34   not yet identified
 abu zufur
  fish from Roman midden. no
   specimen
 bishbish
  conch from Roman midden.
   no specimen

Notes

1. The Desert and Its People

1. Rainfall sometimes is especially abundant in a particular year or for several consecutive years. Muhammad Umbaarak boasted of the 1954 rainfall episode which devastated the city of Qena: "It watered the land from Subayr southward to God knows where. For three years we bathed in the pleasure of this water. Even the Hamadiyiin clan came as far south as Umm Diisa to enjoy the pasture." Exceptionally wet years in Maʿaza territory were, according to Bedouin reports and published sources, 1887, 1926–32, 1951–52, 1955, 1960–61, 1968–70, and 1987–88. Sometimes, however, rain fails over the entire Maʿaza area for years at a time. Exceptionally dry years included 1870–73, 1882–86, 1928–32, 1949–51, 1956–58, and 1977–85. See Floyer (1887, 679); Kassas (1953, 254); Kassas and Zahran (1965, 174); and Russell (1949, 118).

2. The largest of these watercourses are ancient rivers, carved out when the area enjoyed regular and more abundant rainfall (see Kassas and Girgis 1964, 110–112). These piedmont watercourses are the richest natural areas in the Maʿaza desert. A typical association of plants and animals in this habitat is one I observed in Wadi Umm Afraad during a very dry period in which perennials were the dominant flora: the shrubs *Zilla spinosa, Zygophyllum coccineum, Artemisia judaica, Pulicaria undulata, Forskholea tenacissima, Solenostemma arghel, Launea spinosa, Pergularia tomentosa;* the trees *Lycium shawii, Moringa peregrina, Leptadenia pyrotechnica, Periploca aphylla,* and *Acacia raddiana;* the mammals Rueppell's sand fox (*Vulpes rueppelli*), dorcas gazelle (*Gazella dorcas*), and Egyptian spiny mouse (*Acomys cahirinus*); the birds sand partridge (*Ammoperdix heyi*), brown-necked raven (*Corvus ruficollis*), and mourning wheatear (*Oenanthe lugens*); and the reptile Grey's agama (*Agama agama spinosa*); see also Goodman et al. (1988, 58).

3. The nomads do not have terms for annuals and perennials, but readily differentiate which species survive for given periods of time after rain: *Lotononis platycarpa, Tribulus* sp., *Morettia philaena,* and *Pulicaria undulata* which last up to a year after a rainfall event; other "annuals" sometimes continue growing for several years, including *Zilla spinosa, Lotus deserti, Anabasis setifera,* and *Artemisia judaica.* The Bedouins have always insisted, and Western science has only recently verified, that dorcas gazelles thrive without drinking water, satisfying their moisture requirements by eating green plants. Other drought-enduring animals include, ac-

cording to the Khushmaan, the dabb-lizards, hoopoe lark, hare, Barbary sheep, hyrax, and jerboas.

4. The hardiness of perennial plants is illustrated by a dried specimen of *shibrim* (*Convolvulus hystrix*) that I collected in the desert in November 1982 and sent in this condition to California in September 1983. It remained there in a cardboard box in a dark attic until January 1984, when I extracted it and found it had begun sending forth bright green tentacles on what little moisture the air contained.

5. Khushmaan naming reflects the society's patrilineal structure. A man's or woman's surname is the father's first name; thus Saalih calls himself Saalih ʿAli after his father, whose name was ʿAli Suwaylim. People call him either by this name or by Saalih Abuu ʿAli, that is, "Saalih whose father is ʿAli," or Abu ʿIyd, the "Father of ʿIyd," referring to his eldest son.

6. See also Spooner (1971, 203).

7. For other notes on the discrepancies between the ideology of the segmentary lineage system and actual practice, see especially Salzman (1978, 622, 626) and Gellner (1973, 3).

2. Nomads and Neighbors

1. Susan Slyomovics, personal communication. Similarly, it is reported that in the Sudan "Bedouin" or "Arab" connotes an uncouth or barbarian existence; see Mohammed (1973, 107).

3. A Desert Livelihood

1. A similar evaluation of the quality of pastoral nomadic life may be found in Darling and Farvar (1972, 671).

2. Johnson's (1969) scheme sensibly avoids the problems created by rigidly trying to classify any one of the widely varying patterns of pastoral nomadic movement. Classifying types of nomadism is one of the oldest approaches in the literature on pastoral nomadism. See, for example, Dyson-Hudson (1972, 8); Bacon (1954, 54ff.); and Krader (1959, 50iff.).

3. See, for example, E. Marx (1978, 68); Dyson-Hudson (1972, 15, 22); Awad (1954, 247); Mohammed (1973, 108); and N. Swidler (1980, 21).

4. Oxby (1975, 2). This quote is cited in Heady (1972, 692). See also Weissleder (1978, xiii).

5. For discussion of the negative aspects of enforced sedentarization and other antinomad activities, see especially Darling and Farvar (1972, 678) and Asad (1973, 69).

6. For discussion of multiresource nomadism, see Dyson-Hudson (1972, 17) and Salzman (1979).

7. For discussion of the ecological and economic strategies of mixed herding, see Lundholm (1976, 30, 32, 34) and Aronson (1980, 176).

8. The protozoan *Theileria hirci*, carried by the tick *Hyalomma rhipicephaloides*, which has been collected on the east flank of the South Galala Plateau.

9. For a fine discussion of nomads' perceptions of and responses to drought, see Johnson (1973, 3, 14).

10. At the drought's peak in 1984, for example, one-third to one-half of all desert Khushmaan families remained in the desert using these resources, especially in the largest, best-vegetated wadis draining the massif of Gattaar, Jebel Shaayib, and Jebel Abul Hassan. Most other families were camped along the Qena-Safaga road to take advantage of the windfall source of American grain spilled on the roadside.

4. Belongings and Beliefs

1. "Ad-dunya filaahi, was hazuuha malaahi, wa fatuuha hamaa-i."
2. For more information on Khushmaan uses of plants, see Goodman and Hobbs (1988).

5. The Bedouin Landscape

1. The concept of landscape as a "vast mnemonic system" was put forth by Lynch (1960, 126).

6. A Bedouin Natural History

1. The *shiib* is not what Westerners would call mythical, for its appearance and habits are well known to the nomads. It is a doglike creature which the Khushmaan insist is distinct from the hyena, jackal, and domestic dog. While hyenas prey equally upon dogs, donkeys, and sheep, the *shiib* takes sheep, goats, and even camels but shuns dogs and donkeys. In Khushmaan territory the animal appeared once in 1947, when it took several sheep and was seen by Suliman ʿAwda's wife Nuwayjaʿ in Wadi Umm Anfiiʿa, and again in 1985 on the east flank of Jebel Umm ʿAnab, where it took a female goat belonging to Laafiy ʿAyd (see also Tregenza, 1955, 90; Tregenza concluded the Umm Anfiiʿa animal was a jackal). The *shiib* has a longer neck and muzzle than the hyena and a straight back rather than the hyena's sloping back. It is larger and has longer legs than the jackal. Curiously, in Arabia, Alois Musil heard accounts of a bizarre animal also called *shiib* which is a "cross between a wolf and a female hyena . . . and attacks a man even when not provoked" (1928, 122). Perhaps the animal is a wolf (*Canis lupus*), never known with certainty from Egypt but which survives in southwest Asia. The Khushmaan have an aversion to the larger carnivores which was probably typical of man everywhere before he had firearms. The Khushmaan admit without embarrassment that hyenas and jackals prevent them from pasturing their livestock in the Labyrinth and other areas adjacent to the Nile Valley, where these animals are known to prey on sheep, goats, and ibex. They believe, with good reason in view of accounts from Kenya and elsewhere in sub-Saharan Africa, that hyenas will attack living men and eat whatever body parts they can. "People stay together when hyenas are about," Musallim Sulimaan said.

2. A reliable indication of Bedouin familiarity with an animal is the number of terms associated with it. The ibex has almost as many different names for sex, age, and other characteristics as do sheep and goats. These are the principal terms:

Age	Male	Female	Plural
< 1 yr	Asfar	Safraa	
	Jidi	ʿAnaaz	
	ʿAtuut	Rabaʿiyya	
	Zuliit		Zulayyit; Abu Zultaan; Baham as-Sayd
Juvenile	Abu Sadfa		
		ʿArwiyya	ʿArwayii
	Hawli	Hawliyya	
One-span	Abu Shibr		
Two-span	Abu Shibrayn		
Three-span	Abu Thalaatha		
Four-span	Abu Arbaʿ		
Five-span	Abu Khamsa		
Six-span	Abu Sitta		
Adult	Badan		Abduun
		ʿArwiyya	

3. An outsider agrees: "Limestone in fact builds bonny ibex," wrote Owen; "lime is well known medically for its bone-building properties. . . . granite is not noted for vitamins" (1937, 161).

4. The Bedouins responded with laughter to my reading from a wildlife guide that "probably no more than 300 Nubian Ibex" are left in the world (Dorst and Dandelot, 1970, 271).

5. Boulos and Hobbs (1986) discuss some of these relict plants.

6. A study of the cave remains was financed by the National Geographic Society Committee for Research and Exploration, to which the author is grateful. Mr. Steven Goodman, Dr. Douglas Brewer, and I made up the field team.

7. For accounts of long-term environmental change in Egypt, see Butzer (1961, 1976) and Murray (1951).

7. Conservation and Conservatism

1. Similar views of resource destruction by nomads are expressed by Shepard (1967), Brown (1971), and Butzer (1974, 65).

2. The Khushmaan may have fashioned their "lineage preserves" after practices of their ʿAbabda neighbors. Admiring the extensive acacia groves in ʿAbabda wadis, the Khushmaan explain that individual ʿAbabda families long ago assumed responsibility for protecting resources in certain wadis. Eventually, all ʿAbabda territory became a mosaic of places patrolled by ʿAbadi families. This vigilance has produced excellent results, according to the Khushmaan: "The ʿAbabda have many more *sayaal* than we have here, because they decided early it was forbidden to cut them. There are many, many! Within two hundred meters, you can see one thousand *sayaal*. I have seen this, in Wadi Hamamiid, Wadi Khashab, and Wadi Girf. . . . Here, in comparison, there are no *sayaal*." ʿAbabda tree protection seems to date from at least 1912, when the English geographer Ball observed that charcoal

burning "has been practiced, especially in the Ababda country, but is not much carried on now" (1912, 35).

3. For a more detailed discussion of Khushmaan conservation, see Hobbs (1988). While there are other examples of pastoral nomadic groups having practiced some form of resource conservation, such as the *hema* system described in Syria and the Arabian Peninsula (see Draz 1985), these are regarded as historical phenomena that did not withstand the politics and technologies of the twentieth century. A major difference between *hema* and Khushmaan conservation is that the former was a legitimized, routinized method for dealing with the normal environmental pressures of drought and resource shortage and was consistent with traditional patterns of spatial organization and rights to resources in the societies that practiced *hema*. Khushmaan practices, in contrast, are a recent development in response to a particular environmental crisis and involve a number of innovations that reject traditional Khushmaan rules about the relationships between society, territory, and biotic resources.

4. See International Union for the Conservation of Nature and Natural Resources (1980), Baines (1985), and Pitt (1985, 287).

Bibliography

Ali, Maher. 1978. "Why the Antagonistic Attitude towards the Deserts and How to Overcome the Situation." *Egyptian Journal of Wildlife and Natural Resources* 1:7–11.

Allan, W. 1976. *The African Husbandman*. Edinburgh: Oliver and Boyd.

Al-Qaradawi, Yusuf. 1985. *The Lawful and Prohibited in Islam*. London: Shorouk International.

Aronson, Dan R. 1980. "Must Nomads Settle? Some Notes toward Policy on the Future of Nomadism." In *When Nomads Settle*, edited by Philip Carl Salzman, pp. 173–184. New York: J. F. Bergin.

Asad, Talal. 1973. "The Bedouin as a Military Force: Notes on Some Aspects of Power Relations between Nomads and Sedentaries in Historical Perspective." In *The Desert and the Sown: Nomads in the Wider Society*, edited by Cynthia Nelson, pp. 61–74. Berkeley: University of California Institute of International Studies, Research Series No. 21.

Awad, Mohamed. 1954. "The Assimilation of Nomads in Egypt." *Geographical Review* 44:240–252.

Bacon, Elizabeth E. 1954. "Types of Nomadism in Central and Southwest Asia." *Southwestern Journal of Anthropology* 10:44–68.

Baines, Graham. 1985. "Draft Programme on Traditional Knowledge for Conservation." *Tradition, Conservation, and Development* 3:5–13.

Ball, John. 1912. *The Geography and Geology of South-Eastern Egypt*. Cairo: University Press.

Barth, Fredrik. 1961. *Nomads of South Persia: The Basseri Tribe of the Khamseh Confederacy*. New York: Humanities Press.

———. 1962. "Nomadism in the Mountain and Plateau Areas of South-West Asia." In *The Problems of the Arid Zone*. Paris: UNESCO.

Boulos, Loutfy, and Joseph Hobbs. 1986. "Three Arboreal Species New to the Eastern Desert of Egypt." *Candollea* 41:183–191.

Brown, Leslie. 1971. "The Biology of Pastoral Man as a Factor in Conservation." *Biological Conservation* 3(2):93–100.

Budge, E. A. Wallis, trans. 1907. Palladius's *The Paradise, or Garden of the Holy Fathers*. London: Chatto and Windus.

Butzer, Karl W. 1961. "Climatic Change in Arid Regions since the Pliocene." In *A*

History of Land Use in Arid Regions, edited by Lawrence Dudley Stamp, pp. 31–56. Paris: UNESCO Arid Zone Research Vol. 17.

————. 1974. "Accelerated Soil Erosion: A Problem of Man-Land Relationships." In *Perspectives on Environment,* edited by Ian R. Manners and Marvin W. Mikesell, pp. 57–78. Washington, D.C.: Association of American Geographers Commission on College Geography Publication No. 13.

————. 1976. *Early Hydraulic Civilization in Egypt.* Chicago: University of Chicago Press.

Chapman, Margaret. 1985. "Environmental Influences on the Development of Traditional Conservation in the South Pacific Region." *Environmental Conservation* 12 : 217–230.

Cloudsley-Thompson, J. L. 1977. *Man and the Biology of Arid Zones.* Baltimore: University Park Press.

Darling, F. Fraser, and Mary A. Farvar. 1972. "Ecological Consequences of Sedentarization of Nomads." In *The Careless Technology: Ecology and International Development,* edited by M. Taghi Farvar and John Milton, pp. 671–682. New York: Natural History Press.

Dawood, N. J., trans. 1968. *The Koran.* Harmondsworth, Middlesex: Penguin Books.

Dickson, Harold Richard Patrick. 1949. *The Arab of the Desert: A Glimpse into Badawin Life in Kuwait and Sáudi Arabia.* London: Allen and Unwin.

Dorst, Jean, and Pierre Dandelot. 1970. *A Field Guide to the Larger Mammals of Africa.* London: Collins.

Draz, Omar. 1985. "The Hema System of Range Reserves in the Arabian Peninsula: Its Possibilities in Range Improvement and Conservation Projects in the Near East." In *Culture and Conservation: The Human Dimension in Environmental Planning,* edited by Jeffrey A. McNeely and David Pitt, pp. 109–122. Beckenham, Kent: Croom Helm.

Dyson-Hudson, Neville. 1972. "The Study of Nomads." In *Perspectives on Nomadism,* edited by William Irons and Neville Dyson-Hudson, pp. 2–29. Leiden: E. J. Brill.

Floyer, E. A. 1887. "Notes on a Sketch Map of Two Routes in the Eastern Desert of Egypt." *Proceedings of the Royal Geographical Society of London* 9 : 659–681.

Gellner, Ernest. 1973. "Introduction to Nomadism." In *The Desert and the Sown: Nomads in the Wider Society,* edited by Cynthia Nelson, pp. 1–10. Berkeley: University of California Institute of International Studies, Research Series No. 21.

Goodman, Steven M., and Joseph J. Hobbs. 1988. "The Ethnobotany of the Egyptian Eastern Desert: A Comparison of Common Plant Usage between Two Culturally Distinct Bedouin Groups." *Journal of Ethnopharmacology* 23 : 73–89.

Goodman, Steven M., Peter L. Meininger, Sherif M. Baha El Din, Joseph J. Hobbs, and Wim C. Mullie. 1988. *The Birds of Egypt.* Oxford: Oxford University Press.

Heady, Harold F. 1972. "Ecological Consequences of Bedouin Settlement in Saudi Arabia." In *The Careless Technology: Ecology and International Development,* edited by M. Taghi Farvar and John P. Milton, pp. 683–693. New York: Natural History Press.

Heathcote, R. L. 1983. *The Arid Lands: Their Use and Abuse.* New York: Longman.

Hobbs, Joseph J. 1986. "Bedouin Reconciliation with the Egyptian Desert." Ph.D. diss., University of Texas at Austin.

———. 1988. "Bedouin Conservation of Plants and Animals in the Eastern Desert of Egypt." In *Arid Lands Today and Tomorrow: Proceedings of an International Research and Development Conference, Tucson, October 20–25, 1985,* edited by Emily E. Whitehead, Charles F. Hutchinson, Barbara N. Timmermann, and Robert G. Varady, pp. 997–1005. Boulder: Westview Press.

International Union for the Conservation of Nature and Natural Resources. 1980. *World Conservation Strategy.* Gland, Switzerland: IUCN.

Jackson, J. K. 1957. "Changes in Climate and Vegetation of the Sudan." *Sudan Notes and Records* 38 : 47–66.

Johnson, Douglas L. 1969. *The Nature of Nomadism.* Chicago: University of Chicago Department of Geography Research Paper No. 118.

———. 1973. "The Response of Pastoral Nomads to Drought in the Absence of Outside Intervention." New York: United Nations Special Sahelian Office Document ST/SSo/18.

Kassas, M. 1953. "Habitat and Plant Communities in the Egyptian Desert. II. The Features of a Desert Community." *Journal of Ecology* 41 : 248–256.

Kassas, M., and W. A. Girgis. 1964. "Habitat and Plant Communities in the Egyptian Desert. V. The Limestone Plateau." *Journal of Ecology* 52 : 107–119.

———. 1964. "Studies on the Ecology of the Eastern Desert, Egypt. I: The Region between Latitude 27°30′ and Latitude 25°30′N." *Bulletin de la Société de Géographie d'Égypte* 41–42 : 43–72.

Kassas, M., and M. A. Zahran. 1965. "Studies on the Ecology of the Red Sea Coastal Land. II. The District from El-Galala El-Qibliya to Hurghada." *Bulletin de la Société de Géographie d'Égypte* 38 : 155–193.

Kennett, Austin. 1925. *Bedouin Justice: Laws and Customs among the Egyptian Bedouin.* Cambridge: Cambridge University Press.

Konczacki, Z. A. 1978. *The Economics of Pastoralism.* London: Frank Cass.

Krader, Lawrence. 1959. "The Ecology of Nomadic Pastoralism." *International Social Science Journal* 11 : 499–510.

Lee, Richard B. 1968. "What Hunters Do for a Living, or, How to Make Out on Scarce Resources." In *Man the Hunter,* edited by Richard B. Lee and Irven De Vore, pp. 30–48. Chicago: Aldine.

Lundholm, Bengt. 1976. "Domestic Animals in Arid Ecosystems." In *Can Desert Encroachment Be Stopped? A Study with Emphasis on Africa,* edited by Anders Rapp, Henri N. Le Houerou, and Bengt Lundholm, pp. 29–42. Stockholm: Swedish Natural Science Research Council Bulletin No. 24.

Lynch, Kevin. 1960. *The Image of the City.* Cambridge, Mass.: Technology Press and Harvard University Press.

Marx, Emanuel. 1978. "The Ecology and Politics of Nomadic Pastoralists in the Middle East." In *The Nomadic Alternative,* edited by Wolfgang Weissleder, pp. 41–74. The Hague: Mouton.

Marx, Hymen. 1968. *Checklist of the Reptiles and Amphibians of Egypt.* Cairo: Special Publication, United States Medical Research Unit No. 3.

Meigs, Peveril. 1966. *Geography of Coastal Deserts.* Paris: UNESCO Arid Zone Research No. 28.

Mikesell, Marvin W. 1970. "Cultural Ecology." In *Focus on Geography: Key Concepts and Teaching Strategies,* edited by Philip Bacon. Washington, D.C.: National Council for the Social Studies.

Mohammed, Abbas. 1973. "The Nomad and the Sedentary: Polar Complementaries—Not Polar Opposites." In *The Desert and the Sown: Nomads in the Wider Society,* edited by Cynthia Nelson, pp. 97–112. Berkeley: University of California Institute of International Studies, Research Series No. 21.

Murray, George W. 1912. "The Qena-Qoseir Road." *Cairo Scientific Journal* 6(69): 138–142.

———. 1930. "Egyptian Mountains." *Alpine Journal* 42:226–235.

———. 1949. "Desiccation in Egypt." *Société Royale de Géographie d'Égypte* 23(1–2): 19–34.

———. 1950. *Sons of Ishmael: A Study of the Egyptian Bedouin.* New York: Humanities Press, 1950.

———. 1951. "The Egyptian Climate: An Historical Outline." *Geographical Journal* 117:422–434.

———. 1967. *Dare Me to the Desert.* London: Allen and Unwin.

Musil, Alois. 1928. *The Manners and Customs of the Rwala Bedouins.* New York: American Geographical Society Oriental Explorations and Studies No. 6.

Osborn, Dale J., and Ibrahim Helmy. 1980. *The Contemporary Land Mammals of Egypt (Including Sinai).* Chicago: Field Museum of Natural History, Fieldiana Zoology New Series No. 5.

Owen, T. R. H. 1937. "The Red Sea Ibex." *Sudan Notes and Records* 20:159–165.

Oxby, Clare. 1975. *Pastoral Nomads and Development.* London: International African Institute.

Pitt, David. 1985. "Towards Ethnoconservation." In *Culture and Conservation: The Human Dimension in Environmental Planning,* edited by Jeffrey A. McNeely and David Pitt, pp. 283–295. Beckenham, Kent: Croom Helm.

Reed, Charles A. 1977. *Origins of Agriculture.* Chicago: Aldine.

Richards, Paul. 1975. *African Environment.* London: International African Institute.

Robinson, A. E. 1935. "Desiccation or Destruction: Notes on the Increase of Desert Areas in the Nile Valley." *Sudan Notes and Records* 18:119–130.

Russell, Thomas W. 1949. *Egyptian Service, 1902–1946.* London: John Murray.

Salzman, Philip Carl. 1978. "Ideology and Change in Middle Eastern Tribal Societies." *Man,* n.s., 13:618–637.

———. 1979. "Multi-Resource Nomadism in Iranian Baluchistan." In *Perspectives on Nomadism,* edited by William Irons and Neville Dyson-Hudson, pp. 60–68. Leiden: E. J. Brill.

———, ed. 1980. *When Nomads Settle.* New York: J. F. Bergin.

Sauer, Carl O. 1952. *Agricultural Origins and Dispersals.* New York: American Geographical Society.

Schmidt-Nielsen, K. 1964. *Desert Animals: Physiological Problems of Heat and Water.* Oxford: Clarendon Press.

Shepard, Paul. 1967. *Man in the Landscape.* New York: Knopf.

Spooner, Brian. 1971. "Towards a Generative Model of Nomadism." *Anthropological Quarterly* 44:198–210.

———. 1973. *The Cultural Ecology of Pastoral Nomads.* Reading, Mass.: Addison Wesley Modules in Anthropology No. 45.

Sweet, Louise E. 1965. "Camel Raiding of North Arabian Bedouin: A Mechanism of Ecological Adaptation." *American Anthropologist* 67:1132–1150.

Swidler, Nina. 1980. "Sedentarization and Modes of Economic Integration in the Middle East." In *When Nomads Settle,* edited by Philip Carl Salzman, pp. 21–33. New York: J. F. Bergin.

Swidler, W. W. 1973. "Adaptive Processes Regulating Nomad-Sedentary Interaction in the Middle East." In *The Desert and the Sown: Nomads in the Wider Society,* edited by Cynthia Nelson, pp. 23–42. Berkeley: University of California Institute of International Studies, Research Series No. 21.

Tackholm, Vivi. 1974. *Student's Flora of Egypt.* Beirut: Cooperative Printing.

Thirgood, J. V. 1981. *Man and the Mediterranean Forest: A History of Resource Depletion.* New York: Academic Press.

Tregenza, Leon Arthur. 1955. *The Red Sea Mountains of Egypt.* London: Oxford University Press.

———. 1958. *Egyptian Years.* London: Oxford University Press.

Ucko, P. J., and G. W. Dimbleby, eds. 1954. *The Domestication and Exploitation of Plants and Animals.* London: Duckworth.

von Dumreicher, Andre. 1931. *Trackers and Smugglers in the Deserts of Egypt.* New York: Dial Press.

Wahba, Saʿad al-Din. 1967. *Sikka as-Salaama* (in Arabic). Cairo: Daar al-Kitaab al-ʿArabii lil-Tibaaʿa wa al-Nashr.

Watt, J. M., and M. G. Breyer-Brandwijk. 1962. *Medicinal and Poisonous Plants of Southern and Eastern Africa.* London: E. and S. Livingstone.

Wehr, Hans. 1976. *A Dictionary of Modern Written Arabic.* Translated by J. Milton Cowan. Ithaca: Spoken Language Service.

Weigall, Arthur Edward Pierce. 1909. *Travels in Upper Egyptian Deserts.* Edinburgh: Blackwood and Sons.

Weissleder, Wolfgang, ed. 1978. *The Nomadic Alternative.* The Hague: Mouton.

Wilkinson, John. 1832. "Notes on a Part of the Eastern Desert of Upper Egypt." *Journal of the Royal Geographical Society, London* 2:28–60.

Index